JULIUS CAESAR

Cover Illustration: Nancy Peach
Cover Design: Bonni Gatter

High Noon Books
A division of Academic Therapy Publications
20 Commercial Boulevard
Novato, CA 94949-6191

International Standard Book Number: 1-57128-423-0

6 5 4 3 2 1 0 9 8 7
0 9 8 7 6 5 4 3 2 1

Another attractive book in the Streamlined
Shakespeare series is *Romeo and Juliet*. Write or visit
us online to see our entire catalog.
www.HighNoonBooks.com

Table of Contents

ABOUT
WILLIAM SHAKESPEARE
(1564-1616)

William Shakespeare was born in Stratford-upon-Avon, a market town about eighty miles northwest of London. His father was a glovemaker and a trader in wool, hides, and grain. The family, which had eight children, while not rich, led a comfortable life. William was the third child in the family, and it is thought that he attended the Stratford grammar school where classes started at six or seven in the morning and lasted until five or six in the late afternoon. When the family's finances declined, it became necessary for him to leave school to go to work for a local tradesman.

He married Anne Hathaway when he was eighteen and she was twenty-six. They had three children, including twins.

It is not known exactly when or why Shakespeare left Stratford and moved to London where he quickly became involved in the theater both as an actor and a playwright. Theaters in London were closed from 1592 to 1594 because of the terrifying plague that swept throughout Europe, so Shakespeare spent his time writing plays and publishing two long narrative poems that immediately became popular and started him on the road to fame.

We can tell from the records of the number of properties he bought in London and Stratford that his income was more than ample. His days were busy acting

v

at the Blackfriar and Globe Theaters and writing new plays to be performed there.

Shakespeare was only fifty-two when he died in Stratford. His birthplace and Anne Hathaway's cottage have been furnished to look as much as possible as they did in Shakespeare's time and are visited by thousands of tourists and admirers each year.

To this day Shakespeare's works can be found on stages in every country in the world. The work of no other playwright has been performed in so many nations throughout so many centuries. His friend Ben Johnson wrote in 1623, "He was not of an age, but for all of time." By now we know Johnson's observation was absolutely correct!

JULIUS CAESAR

THE STORY

Prologue

This is not a story about the great Julius Caesar. In fact, he has but a minor role in the play that bears his name. It is a story about a bloody struggle for power—a struggle between power for one and power for all. Would Rome become a monarchy or remain a democracy? Tyranny, jealousy, and love of freedom set the stage for a chain of violent acts. A great leader falls victim to his own vanity. An honorable man loses all when he becomes a murderer. Chaos rules as revenge is sought. And the reader must decide who are the true heroes and who are the traitors in this tragic tale.

Act I
Scene 1

Our story takes place in Rome where the great Julius Caesar ruled. On this bright morning, a crowd of tradesmen and other commoners gathered in the city square to celebrate. Caesar had won an important military victory. He had defeated the army of Pompey's sons. Caesar was a very popular ruler who was particularly admired by the lower classes. The happy group sang praises of Caesar and his victory. They danced in the street. And they decorated statues of Caesar with crowns. As the crowd celebrated, two Roman tribunes came around the corner to witness the noisy scene. The tribunes, Flavius and Marullus, were not pleased with the sight.

"You idle creatures, get you home!" shouted Flavius, "Is this a holiday? Where are your work clothes? You know you shouldn't be walking around without the signs of your trade on a workday." Then he singled out one of the commoners.

"What is your trade?" Flavius asked.

"Why, sir, a carpenter," the man answered.

"Where is your leather apron and ruler?" asked Marullus. "Why are you wearing your best clothes?"

Then Marullus eyed another commoner. "You, sir, what trade are you?"

"I am a cobbler," answered the man with a sly grin.

"But why aren't you in your shop today?" asked

Flavius. "Why are you leading these men around the streets when you should be working?"

"Well, sir," the cobbler answered, "I want to wear out their shoes so I can get more work." He pointed to the shoes of those around him. Laughter broke out in the group. Flavius and Marullus frowned at the crowd.

"Truly, sir, we are taking a holiday to see Caesar," said the cobbler. "We want to celebrate his triumph."

"There is nothing to celebrate today," shouted Marullus. He remembered the many times that these same men had celebrated Pompey's victories. The crowds had shouted so loudly that the Tiber River trembled. Now these shortsighted men were eager to celebrate the fall of Pompey's sons.

"You fools, you hard-hearted men of Rome," cried Marullus. "Cannot you remember the great Pompey and the many times you cheered for him? Now you put on your best clothes and call this a holiday? Be gone! Run to your houses. Fall upon your knees. Pray to the gods that a plague will not be sent to punish you."

"Go now, good countrymen," added Flavius. "Go to the banks of the Tiber and weep your tears into the river."

The crowd was now somber. The older ones hung their heads. Marullus' words brought back memories. It was true. Many times in the past they had gathered their entire families to watch Pompey march through these streets. They had told their children stories of the bravery of Pompey's soldiers. Today they were celebrating his defeat. Marullus was right to remind them of Pompey's noble history. Caesar's greatness had blinded them. His light was so bright that it was hard to see past the glow. These were the thoughts of many in the crowd as they retreated down the alleys out of the square.

The younger men in the crowd followed the lead of their elders, but they had different thoughts. They did not want to fight the tribunes with their swords. Yet they would have their day. They would bask in the glory of Caesar's victorious return to Rome. No one could stop them, not even the tribunes. They would retreat, for now, but they would return.

Satisfied that they had scattered the crowd, Flavius said to Marullus, "See how tongue-tied they become in their guilt? Let's now go in different directions. Let us take the decorations off all statues of Caesar."

"Do you think that we should do this?" asked Marullus. "You know it is the feast of Lupercal." He thought it a bad idea to do anything disrespectful to Caesar during the feast.

"It doesn't matter," answered Flavius. "We can't let any images of Caesar be decorated. He is an ordinary man."

Above all, Flavius felt that it was important that Caesar should not be honored in such a way that placed him over other men. This was tyranny.

"We cannot have one man soaring above all others," said Flavius.

Marullus nodded and the men departed. Each left with a mission. They would preserve the Republic of Rome at all costs. Power must be shared. If Caesar became king, he would have all of the power. His ambition must not go unchecked.

Act I
Scene 2

I n spite of the tribunes' efforts, the crowds could not be dispersed. The tribunes chased men up and down narrow alleys and through courtyards. They shouted for the commoners to return to their homes. Each time they felt they were making progress, they would turn a corner to find another crowd of people waiting for Caesar. The people hung from balconies. They strained to see from windows. All Rome waited. They would not be deprived of celebrating their hero.

Finally Caesar came. The uproar was deafening. The crowd cried out in admiration as their great leader and his wife, Calpurnia, made their way into the city square. Caesar's friend, Antony, followed closely behind. Antony's eyes were firmly fixed on the man he idolized.

"Calpurnia!" called Caesar.

"Quiet, everyone. Caesar speaks," said Casca, who was one of his strongest supporters. Behind his back, some referred to Casca as Caesar's lap dog.

"Here, my lord," answered Calpurnia. Long dark tresses framed her once beautiful face. She had been the fairest beauty in all of Rome when Caesar had married her. But that was long ago. Now her beauty had faded. The shadow of age grew long on her striking features.

"Calpurnia, don't forget to stand directly in Antony's way when he runs," reminded Caesar. "And Antonio, don't forget to touch Calpurnia. Our elders have said that women who have not children can shake off their sterile curse if touched by the runner."

Calpurnia bowed her head to her husband. Although her face was lowered, it was easy to see the fiery blush of her cheeks. The great Caesar needed an heir. His wife had been unable to provide one. Everyone assumed she was at fault as no one could imagine that Caesar could fail at anything. Calpurnia indeed believed this, also. Thus, she was filled with shame for her failure.

"I shall remember," said Antony. "When Caesar says do something, it is done." Caesar's wishes were Antony's commands.

Antony stood tall in the square. Boldly he began stripping off his clothes. The feast of Lupercal required a chosen man to run a naked foot-race through the streets of Rome. Being handsome and athletic, Antony was the honored runner.

"Go now, Antonio," commanded Caesar. But before Antony could begin, a cry was heard from the crowd.

"Caesar!" someone cried out loudly.

"Who is calling me?" asked Caesar. "I hear a very shrill tongue calling me." His eyes searched the sea of faces.

"Beware the ides of March," croaked the strange voice.

"Who is that?" asked Caesar.

"It's just a soothsayer who tells you to beware the ides of March," said Brutus. He was a senator and a close friend to Caesar.

"Let me see him," said Caesar. "Bring him to me."

Cassius went into the crowd as Caesar bid. The crowd parted to expose an old man. He was standing alone in the midst of the crowd that looked on suspiciously. Cassius brought the man before Caesar.

The weird voice came from a man with an eerie

presence. His clothes were disheveled. His white hair was like a ball of dandelion fuzz. He leaned his sparse frame against a tree branch, which he used for a walking stick. His eyes were milky blue mirrors. And he moved forward as if in a trance.

"What did you say to me?" asked Caesar. "Say it again."

"Beware the ides of March," the old man called out again.

Caesar looked the man over. The crowd was silent. Caesar's gaze was like a searchlight. His eyes ran up and down the man. Then he turned away.

"He is a dreamer," said Caesar. "Let us leave him." With that, Caesar led the way to the festival. The admiring crowd followed.

Brutus and Cassius, another senator, stayed behind. They were weary of following Caesar's every step. The two men fell into quiet conversation. Cassius mentioned that lately Brutus had not seemed very friendly. Brutus assured Cassius that he was not angry with him. He said that recently he had been having some troubling feelings. He was preoccupied with these. Suddenly there was shouting in the distance.

"I wonder what all the shouting is about?" asked Brutus. "I fear that the people have chosen Caesar for their king." He shook his head sadly.

"Do you fear that?" asked Cassius cautiously. He didn't want to say too much. He wasn't sure how Brutus felt about Caesar's growing power in the Republic.

"I love Caesar well, but I would not have him for a king," answered Brutus. He studied Cassius' face. "Is there something that you want to tell me?"

"I know that you are virtuous, Brutus," said Cassius, "and honor is the subject of my story." He began to tell Brutus of a time that Caesar had challenged Cassius to swim the Tiber River. He had jumped in after Caesar. The two had battled the tide to win the race. But before the men could reach the other side, Caesar began to have trouble. He cried out to Cassius that he would drown if Cassius did not help him. Caesar was like a weakling.

"How is such a man a god?" asked Cassius. Before he could say more another roar of the crowd was heard.

"Is that shout for new honors heaped upon Caesar?" asked Brutus.

"Why does he walk like a giant, while we petty men walk under his huge legs?" asked Cassius. "The fault lies not in the stars, but in ourselves."

Brutus sighed deeply. "I understand what you are saying, Cassius. I will talk with you more later, but not now," said Brutus sadly. The truth was that he could not bear to consider the solution. He loved Caesar. Yet he loved Rome more.

Cassius' heart began to beat wildly. His words had found their target. Brutus had not scorned him. Caesar's noble friend had not shut the door in his face. This was very promising!

The two men could speak no more because Caesar and the crowd entered the square. It appeared that something had happened. Caesar was angry. Calpurnia was pale and shaken. Cicero, a powerful senator, seemed to be enraged.

As Caesar gazed scornfully at the crowd, he appeared to have focused on Cassius. "Antony," Caesar said, "let me have men about me who are fat. Cassius has a lean and hungry look. He thinks too much. Such men are dangerous."

Antony protested that Cassius was a noble Roman. Caesar disagreed, saying that Cassius should be feared. He complained that Cassius didn't like music or plays and seldom smiled. Caesar thought such men were never at peace with themselves. He made Caesar uncomfortable. But the great Caesar did not fear Cassius.

"For always, I am Caesar," he said. Such a great man could not be threatened by other men. With those words, Caesar departed for home with his followers.

As Caesar was leaving, Brutus asked Casca why Caesar looked so sad. He wanted to know what happened at the festival to change Caesar's mood.

"Well, Antony offered Caesar a crown," began Casca. "It wasn't really a crown, just a wreath. Caesar brushed it aside, but I think he really wanted it. Then Antony offered it to him again. He still wouldn't take it. When Antony offered it to Caesar a third time, Caesar refused it. The crowd went wild because Caesar refused the crown three times. Caesar fainted and fell down."

"Caesar fell down?" asked Cassius.

"He fell down in the marketplace and foamed at the mouth," said Casca.

"He has the falling sickness," explained Brutus. "What did he say when he came to?"

"He told the crowd that if he had done or said anything amiss, it was because of his illness," said Casca.

"Did Cicero say anything?" asked Cassius.

"Ay, he spoke Greek," said Casca.

"Well, what did he say?" asked Cassius.

"All I can say is that those that understood him smiled at one another and shook their heads," said Casca, "but it was Greek to me." Then Casca reported that Marullus and Flavius had been sentenced to death for pulling decorations off Caesar's statues.

"Will you have supper with me tonight, Casca?" asked Cassius. There were other things he wanted to discuss.

"No, I cannot tonight," said Casca.

"What about tomorrow night?" asked Cassius.

"If I am still alive and your dinner is worth eating," said Casca.

"Good. I will expect you," said Cassius.

"And I will also leave you," said Brutus. "Tomorrow I will come to your home if you would like to speak with me. Or you can come to my home."

Cassius agreed to meet with Brutus. After Brutus left, Cassius thought about their conversation. He now felt that Brutus could be convinced to join forces with him. He decided on a plan. He would write notes in different handwriting styles. These notes would say that Rome had a very high opinion of Brutus. The notes would also mention Caesar's ambition. These would be thrown through Brutus' window. Surely this would urge Brutus to action. Brutus would feel responsible for checking Caesar's hunger for power!

"Let Caesar be shaken from his seat of power," said Cassius as he gazed at the moon. Rome's future would not be left to fate.

Act I
Scene 3

White veins of lightning brutally pierced the inky sky while thunderbolts crashed. Gusts of wild wind chased leaves and branches through the streets. Trees bent violently to the push of the untamed storm. Owls hooted and frightened children cried. It was an unnatural night that shook the earth. Something was terribly wrong.

As Cicero was making his way home, he came upon Casca.

"Good evening, Casca," cried out Cicero. "Why are you so breathless?"

"Are you not frightened by this dreadful storm?" asked Casca in amazement. "It would seem that there must be a civil war in heaven to cause such destruction."

"What have you seen that is so strange?" asked Cicero.

"I saw a slave who held up his left hand, which burst into flames," said Casca. "Yet, his hand was unscorched when the fire went out! Then I saw a lion that stared at me, but ran off without attacking. Yesterday an owl sat in the square in the middle of day hooting and shrieking. Don't tell me these things are natural, for I believe they are bad omens."

"Indeed, it is strange, but these things happen," answered Cicero. "And men interpret these according to their own ideas. These are different from their true meaning." Cicero was untroubled by the storm and the strange things that Casca described.

"Is Caesar coming to the Capitol tomorrow?" he asked to change the subject.

"He is," said Casca. "He told Antony to tell you he would be there."

"Good night then," said Cicero. "We shouldn't be walking under this disturbed sky."

Casca bid good night to Cicero and wandered on through the town until he came upon Cassius.

"What a night this is," Casca said to Cassius.

"It is a very pleasing night to honest men," said Cassius.

"Who could ever think that the heavens could be so menacing," said Casca. He truly was frightened. He knew that he should go home, but something kept him out. Perhaps it was because he had never seen such a storm in his life.

"I have walked the streets this dangerous night with my robe open," said Cassius. "I have bared my chest to the thunderbolt. I have stood in the path of the blue lightning."

"Why tempt the heavens?" asked Casca.

"Casca, you are pale with fright from the fires, birds and beasts," said Cassius. "I can give you the name of a man who is like this dreadful night. You should fear this monster of a man and what he has become."

" 'Tis Caesar that you mean, is it not, Cassius?" asked Casca.

"Let it be who it is," said Cassius. "Romans seem to have lost our fathers' spirits. We are now governed by our mothers' womanish ways."

"Indeed they say that the senators will establish Caesar as their king tomorrow," said Casca.

"I know where I will wear my dagger then," said

Cassius. He pulled his dagger from its sheath and pretended to stab himself in the heart.

"So will I," said Casca. "As long as we have our daggers we cannot be held captive. If you mount a rebellion to set things right, I will be with you."

"Casca, you should know that some of the noblest men in Rome have vowed to end this tyrant's rule," said Cassius.

Just then, Cinna approached them. He was walking very quickly.

"Where are you going in such haste?" asked Cassius.

"To find you," said Cinna. "What a fearful night this is!"

"Are the others waiting for me?" asked Cassius.

"Yes, they are," answered Cinna. "Oh, Cassius, if you could win the noble Brutus to our cause…"

"I have a plan," said Cassius. Then he told Cinna to take the three notes to Brutus' home. He was to throw these through a window. When Cinna had finished this, he would meet the others at Pompey's Theater. Decius Brutus and Trebonius were to be there also. Cinna left to carry out the instructions.

"Come, Casca, you and I will go to see Brutus at his house," said Cassius. "He's three quarters ours. We will soon have him all."

"He sits high in the people's hearts," said Casca. "We must have him on our side."

Cassius agreed that Brutus must join forces with them. It was the only way. Brutus' honor was essential to their cause. His reputation would soften the blow that would inevitably be dealt to the great Caesar.

Act II
Scene 1

Brutus paced in his garden. He had been unable to sleep. He had tossed and turned in his bed with unsettling thoughts. He tried to tell the time by looking at the stars, but he could not. Brutus called his servant Lucius to light his study so he could work. As he waited for his servant to return, he thought about Caesar.

"For my part, I have no reason to wish his death," Brutus spoke aloud. "And yet, perhaps it must be done for the welfare of the state. If he is crowned, his nature will surely be changed. He will climb the ladder of ambition without regard for the people."

Lucius entered the garden to tell Brutus that the candle in the study was lit.

"I also found this note on your window while I was searching for a flint to light the candle," said Lucius. He handed the paper to his master.

"Get to bed again," said Brutus. "It is not yet day." Then a thought came to him. "Boy, is tomorrow the ides of March?"

"I know not, sir," answered the young servant.

"Look at the calendar and tell me," said Brutus. Were the soothsayer's words connected to his thoughts of Caesar's death? As he looked up, he saw bright lights. Meteorites were blazing through the night sky. There was so much light that he could read by the glow.

The note that Lucius had given him said:

"Brutus, you sleep when you should be awake! Speak! Strike! Set things right! Shall Rome stand under one man's awe?"

Lucius entered the room again. He announced, "Sir, fifteen days have passed in March."

"'Tis good," answered Brutus. "Go to the door. Someone knocks."

Brutus pondered the date. Was this a coincidence? Ever since Cassius had spoken against Caesar, he had thought of little else. Was Caesar's death the answer? If in fact the future of the Republic rested on his shoulders, Brutus knew he must rise to the challenge. But if the Republic was not in danger, Caesar should not be harmed. He felt as if his mind was at war with itself.

"'Tis your brother-in-law, Cassius, at the door," said Lucius returning. "There are also other men with him."

"Do you know them?" asked Brutus.

"No, sir," said Lucius. "Their hats are pulled down. And their faces are buried in their cloaks."

"Let them enter," said Brutus. He knew by Lucius' description that Cassius had brought other conspirators. These men would hide their faces under cover of night. They were ashamed even in the darkness of the night.

A group of men with dark cloaks entered the room. They walked with purpose in their steps. Almost in unison, they dropped their cloaks and showed their faces. Cassius introduced them as Casca, Decius, Cinna, Metellus, and Trebonius. Brutus welcomed them. Cassius asked for a private word with Brutus. The two talked for a few minutes in the corner of the room. When they returned to the group, the expression on Brutus' face was resolute. The men knew that he was on their side!

"Give me your hands, one by one," said Brutus.

24

"And let us swear our resolution," said Cassius.

"No, not an oath," said Brutus. "We are Romans. We have given our word of honor. That is enough."

"What of Cicero?" asked Cassius. "I think he will stand very strong with us."

The others agreed that Cicero would be a strong ally. He was a senator who was a respected elder. This could be most helpful to the cause. Most of the conspirators were young. But Brutus protested. He said that Cicero would not go along with any plan that he did not think of himself. So the others quickly changed their opinion. Whatever Brutus said was accepted. After all, the plan could not go forward without the honorable Brutus.

"Should anyone besides Caesar be touched?" asked Decius. His question was well put. He was really asking whether anyone else should be murdered.

"That is a good question, Decius," said Cassius. "I don't think that it is right that Mark Antony, so well beloved of Caesar, should outlive him. He will make trouble. Let Antony and Caesar fall together."

"Our course would seem too bloody," protested Brutus. "To cut the head off and then hack the limbs would show anger. Antony is but a limb of Caesar. Let's be sacrificers, but not butchers."

"Yet, I fear him because of the love he bears to Caesar," said Cassius.

"Do not think of him, good Cassius," said Brutus. "If he loves Caesar, all he can do is to die for Caesar. And that is unlikely as he is given to sports, wildness, and women."

The sound of a clock was heard. It struck three times. Each strike sent a chill through the men. The time for talking was done. It would soon be time for the deed.

"'Tis time to depart," said Trebonius quietly.

Before leaving, the men expressed some concerns.

What if Caesar did not come to the Senate? Lately he had become very superstitious. The terrible storm and the soothsayer's predictions might keep him home. Decius told the men not to worry. He could persuade Caesar to come. Then it was agreed. All should meet at Caesar's home at eight o'clock in the morning. Together they would bring him to the Capitol. Nothing could be left to chance.

Before the men left, Metellus suggested they bring one more man into the group. He recommended Ligarius, who hated Caesar. Caesar had berated him for speaking well of Pompey. Brutus agreed. Metellus would send Ligarius to Brutus, who would convince him to join their cause.

With that the men departed and Brutus was once again left alone with his thoughts. He looked up at the purple sky that was now still. The wild storm had passed. He stared intently into the night as though he were looking for some sort of sign. Brutus did not hear his wife's softly falling footsteps. He was startled when she touched his arm.

"Brutus, my lord," she said. Her face was marked with distress.

"Portia, why are you up at this hour?" he asked. "It is not good for your health."

"Nor for yours either," she answered. And then she poured forth her feelings as she could no longer restrain them. Her words flowed like a river of pain. Tears fell quietly down her cheeks. She told him that he had recently been so unlike the man she had married. Last night at dinner he had left in the middle of the meal. Tonight he left his bed. He was cross and impatient with her. She had asked him many times what was wrong, but he had refused to confide in her. Portia knew that something was dreadfully wrong.

"My dear lord," she begged, "make me acquainted with your cause of grief."

Brutus could not tell his wife what he was planning. He did not want her to shoulder the burden of the conspiracy. He wanted to protect her.

"I am not well," he said. He tried to sound convincing, but he knew that Portia would not believe him. And she did not.

"If Brutus were sick, he would not get out of bed and walk around in the cold night," she said. She fell to her knees in front of him. "My Brutus, you have some sickness in your mind. As your wife, I should know of it," she said. The tears rushed down her cheeks as she searched her husband's face for clues.

"By all your vows of love and that great vow that did make us one, please tell me why you are so sad," Portia begged. "I saw the men who came to the house. I know they were hiding their faces." She cradled her head in her hands.

"Oh, gentle Portia," said Brutus, "do not kneel." He tried to pull her up.

"I should not need to if you were gentle, Brutus," said Portia. And she begged him to confide in her. She reminded him that marriage required the sharing of confidences.

Brutus took pity on his beautiful wife. He loved her dearly. As her pale hair reflected the light of the moon, her heart reflected purity and love.

"You are my true and honorable wife," he said. He clasped her small hands and kissed them gently.

"If this were true, then I should know this secret," she said. "I grant I am a woman, but I am Brutus' wife and Cato's daughter," Portia reminded him. "Don't you think I am stronger than most women?"

She parted her gown to reveal a bloody wound on

her thigh. The blood ran down to her ankle. Brutus let out a gasp.

"I gave myself this wound to prove my loyalty to you," Portia said. She looked defiantly into his eyes.

"Oh, render me worthy of this noble wife," said Brutus.

Then a sharp knock sounded at the door.

"Portia, go in awhile and I will join you soon," said Brutus. "I will tell you the secrets of my heart."

Portia squeezed his hand. She left to wait for his explanation. Brutus' servant brought Caius Ligarius to him. Brutus asked for his support. But he did not tell him everything.

"And with a heart newly fired, I follow you," said Ligarius. "I know not what I am to do, but it is enough that Brutus leads me."

"Follow me, then," said Brutus.

Brutus ached inside. This desperate deed would not go forward without him. Everything rested on his shoulders.

Act II
Scene 2

C aesar's home had not escaped the violent storm of the evening. It had terrorized his wife. She was tormented by nightmares. Three times Calpurnia had awakened. Each time, she had cried out, "Help, they murder Caesar!"

Caesar asked a servant to go to the priests to make a sacrifice. Surely the gods could stop the chaos. When Calpurnia awoke in the morning, she told Caesar he must not leave the house for the day. Caesar dismissed her concerns, telling her that she had nothing to be worried about. But Calpurnia was firm.

"Caesar, I never paid attention to omens," she said, "but now they frighten me." She recounted the terrible events that were reported of the stormy night. Graves had opened. Corpses had walked free. Fiery warriors had fought in the clouds. Blood had drizzled down on the Capitol. Ghosts shrieked. Dying men groaned. It was more than poor Calpurnia could bear!

Caesar tried to comfort her. He told her that no one knew what these signs meant. Calpurnia was sure that they were meant for Caesar.

"When beggars die, there are no comets," said Calpurnia. "But when a prince dies, the heavens blaze."

"Cowards die many times before their deaths," said Caesar. "The valiant never taste of death but once." It always seemed strange to Caesar that men should fear death. It was an inescapable part of life. A necessary end. Death would come when it came.

Even though Caesar was philosophical about death, he was not above consulting fortune-tellers. Every morning he sent a servant to consult with the soothsayers. This morning his servant returned saying that Caesar should not venture forth today. The priests had sacrificed an animal that was found to have no heart. This was a very bad omen.

"The gods do this to shame cowardice," said Caesar. "Caesar would be a beast without a heart if he should stay at home today for fear. No, Caesar shall not."

"Do not go forth today," Calpurnia said. "Call it *my* fear that keeps you in the house." And then she begged him to send Mark Antony to the Senate to report that Caesar was not well today.

Caesar looked at his wife with exasperation. But his expression softened when their eyes met. He loved Calpurnia. It was hard for him to deny this woman anything.

"Mark Antony shall say I am not well," said Caesar with a long sigh. "For you, I will stay home."

Calpurnia rushed to him. She embraced her husband. She lived in the shadow of this great man. He was her entire life. Life without him would be no life.

Their embrace was interrupted by Decius' entrance. When Caesar told him that he would not come to the Senate today, Decius was visibly shaken. Yet he quickly regained his composure. His mission was to bring Caesar to the Senate. He must not fail! He must think of a way.

"Most mighty Caesar," Decius began, "Let me know some cause, or I will be laughed at."

"The cause is my will," thundered Caesar. "I will not come. That is enough to satisfy the Senate." Then he softened. Decius was a favorite of his. He owed him the truth. Caesar explained that Calpurnia had a dream. In this dream, blood spouted from a hundred holes in a statue of Caesar. Smiling Romans dipped their hands in the blood.

Decius thought quickly. He explained that Calpurnia had misinterpreted the dream. It really meant that Caesar's blood had revived Rome. Caesar considered this idea. Yes, it made perfect sense!

Decius told Caesar there was another reason he must come to the Senate today. Caesar was to be offered a crown. If the senators were told that he could not come because of his wife's dream, they might change their minds.

"If Caesar hides himself, shall they not whisper that he is afraid?" asked Decius.

It did not take long for those words to sink in.

"How foolish do your fears seem now, Calpurnia?" asked Caesar. "I am ashamed I did yield to them. Give me my robe."

Decius was relieved. His plan had worked. Before he had time to congratulate himself for his quick thinking, his fellow conspirators came into the room. Caesar was pleased to see they had come to escort him. He was excited about the crown. It was now within his reach!

"Good friends, let us go in. Have some wine with me. Then we'll leave together like friends," said the jovial Caesar.

Brutus grew uncomfortable as Caesar's mood elevated. Caesar was so trusting of this group of men who presented themselves as friends.

"But we're not like friends, are we?" thought Brutus as he stared at Caesar surrounded by the band of conspirators. Brutus' heart became heavy as he thought of what was to come.

Act II
Scene 3

O n a side street near the Capitol, a man stood in the sunlight reading from a scroll.

Caesar, beware of Brutus. Take heed of Cassius. Come not near Casca. Have an eye on Cinna. Trust not Trebonius or Metellus Cimber. Decius loves you not. Thou hast wronged Caius Ligarius. There is but one mind of all these men and it is bent against Caesar. The mighty gods defend thee.

One who loves you,
Artemidorus.

Artemidorus had heard talk about the conspiracy. He wasn't sure it was true. But he did not want to take any chances. He admired Caesar above all men. He sought to warn him if there was danger ahead.

His plan was to wait for Caesar to pass by on his way to the Senate. He would then give him the scroll. Hopefully Caesar would read the warning. If there was truth to what he had heard, Caesar would be safe. If Caesar did not read the scroll, then fate was a partner in the conspiracy.

He waited impatiently in the morning sun to warn the mighty Caesar.

Act II
Scene 4

Portia was quite upset. She knew that Brutus was involved in something dangerous. But what was it? Though he had promised to confide in her, he had not. A parade of visitors had occupied his attention most of the night. She had fallen asleep waiting for him. And Brutus had left this morning without waking her. Portia decided to send Lucius to the Capitol to find out what was happening.

"Boy, run to the Senate," said Portia. Then she became lost in thought. What was Brutus planning? The boy looked up at her. "Why do you stay?" she asked him impatiently.

The boy was confused. "To know my errand," said Lucius.

"Go there and come back quickly," said Portia. "It would take me too long to explain to you what to do."

"Run to the Capitol and nothing else?" asked Lucius.

"Bring me word if my lord looks well," said Portia. "He was sick this morning. What is that noise?"

"I hear nothing, madam," said Lucius.

The same soothsayer who had warned Caesar about the ides of March walked by the house. Portia asked him where he was going. He said that he wanted to see Caesar as he passed by on the way to the Senate. He was looking for a good place to stand so that he could talk to Caesar as he passed.

"What do you have to say to Caesar that is so

33

important?" asked Portia.

"I shall tell him to look after himself," said the soothsayer.

"Why? Do you know if some harm is intended for him?" asked Portia.

"None that I know of for sure," said the man. "But there is much to fear," he added.

Portia's anxiety was growing. She must find out what was happening. She felt that she would faint in the street if she didn't get some information.

"Lucius, run to the Senate. Tell my lord that I am merry," said Portia. "And then come back and tell me what he said to you."

The young servant thought that his mistress was having some kind of mental breakdown. He was embarrassed at the thought of having to stand in front of his master and report that his wife was merry. He looked at his mistress who was not her usual calm self. She pursed her lips tightly and strained to see down the street. Lucius sighed. He turned and headed for the Senate.

Act III
Scene 1

The conspirators were making their way to the Senate with Caesar. The soothsayer was following close behind. He was desperately trying to talk to Caesar. But the men were closely guarding him. Finally Caesar noticed him.

"The ides of March are come," Caesar said with a slight grin. He wanted the soothsayer to know that his prediction was untrue. He felt especially confident this morning.

"Ay, Caesar," answered the soothsayer, "but they have not gone."

Caesar frowned. Before he could respond, Artemidorus pushed a scroll in front of him.

"Hail, Caesar," said Artemidorus. "Read my suit. It is important to Caesar."

"What matters to me should be read last," scolded Caesar. He waved the man away.

"Delay not, Caesar," Artemidorus urged him. "Read it instantly!"

"Is this fellow mad?" asked Caesar. He again waved the man away. He refused to even look at Artemidorus. "I don't read petitions in the street. Come to the Capitol."

Artemidorus fell back into the crowd. It was hopeless. Nothing could save Caesar. He had tried his best. The conspirators would never let his petition be read in the Senate building.

Caesar and the traitors made their way up the steps of the Capitol. A filtered ray of light lit a path on the steps. As Caesar led the group, it appeared that he was following a golden path. Then a shadow was cast across the steps and the golden path dissolved.

Metellus was the first to present a petition to Caesar. He asked that his exiled brother be returned to Rome. He fell to his knees. He begged Caesar to repeal his brother's banishment. Caesar scolded him for begging. One by one, the conspirators were on their knees to join in the appeal.

An unknowing observer to this scene would have remarked that the circle of men around Caesar appeared to be honoring him. The light from the dome fell on Caesar's head while he spoke. He appeared every inch a leader among men. Caesar was bathed in a warm radiant glow. He stood firm in his resolve.

The clouds above the dome moved to cover the sun. The royal glow was extinguished for a moment. And in this fleeting moment, Casca rose from behind with a blade in his hand.

"Speak, hands, for me!" Casca cried out as he sunk the knife into Caesar's back.

One by one each of the traitors approached Caesar to stab him. Time stood still as Caesar accepted the blows. He did not cry out. Brutus was the last. For an instant he paused. He remembered his love for this man who had long been his friend. Killing Caesar was the greatest sacrifice that he had ever made.

Caesar moved toward Brutus as if to seek protection. Brutus moved forward with purpose. His blade also entered the body of his friend.

"*Et tu, Brute?*" asked Caesar as he mournfully looked into his eyes. "Then, fall, Caesar!" he whispered as his body slipped to the floor. It lay in a bloody pool at the foot of the statue of Pompey.

"Liberty! Freedom! Tyranny is dead!" shouted Cinna. "Run and cry it in the streets!"

The men were jubilant. The bloody deed was done. They plotted their next course of action. Many of the senators had run from the building. Word would soon be in the streets. The people of Rome must understand that Caesar was killed to pay ambition's debt. The conspirators would take full responsibility for the murder. Brutus told the conspirators to dip their hands in Caesar's blood. Then on to the market place, with bloody hands waving like flags, they would cry, "Peace, freedom, and liberty!"

As the men prepared to leave for the market place, Antony's servant entered the room. He was shocked at the ghastly scene. The servant fell to the ground. He spoke in a trembling voice.

"Mark Antony told me to fall down and say, *'Brutus is noble, wise, valiant and honest. Caesar was mighty, bold, royal and loving. If Brutus will promise Mark Antony safety, he will come to find out why Caesar deserved to die.'*"

Brutus assured the servant of his master's safety. He would not be touched. When the servant left, Brutus told the men that Antony would be their friend. The others were not convinced. They did not trust Antony.

When Antony appeared, he ran to the body of his beloved Caesar. He was filled with despair over the loss of his friend. He could not believe that the great Caesar lived no more. Then he turned to the conspirators.

"If I must die," said Antony, "no time would be more fitting than the hour of Caesar's death. No place would please me so as here by Caesar."

"Oh, Antony," said Brutus, "beg not your death of us." Brutus above all did not want any more blood to be shed. "Though now we must appear bloody and cruel, you do not see our hearts." Brutus tried to explain that the murder of Caesar was a necessity. A wrong had been righted. It was all done for the good of the State. Brutus said that he would later tell Antony what had driven him to kill a man he loved so much.

"I doubt not your wisdom," said Antony. But the expression on his face suggested he might not be telling the truth. One by one, he shook the bloody hands of each murderer. As he did so, he professed his love for Caesar. Cassius then asked Antony if they could depend upon him. Antony replied that he must first be told how Caesar presented such a danger to the State.

"Our reasons were so solid," said Brutus "that if you were the son of Caesar, you should be satisfied."

Antony asked permission to carry Caesar's body to the marketplace and speak at his funeral. Brutus agreed. But Cassius was concerned. He drew Brutus aside.

"Brutus, you do not know what you are doing," whispered Cassius. "Do not consent to let Antony speak at his funeral."

Cassius felt it was a bad idea. There was no way to tell what Antony would say to the people. But Brutus would not be swayed. He insisted that he would talk first. He would explain Caesar's death. Then he would permit Antony to speak. Caesar must be given all of the proper funeral rites. Brutus suggested that this would all be to their advantage.

"I know not what may fall," said Cassius, "but I like it not."

Brutus insisted that Antony take Caesar's body. But he warned him not to blame the conspirators in the funeral speech. He was to speak only good of Caesar. He must also say that his funeral speech was permitted by the conspirators. If Antony did not agree to these conditions, he would have no role in the funeral.

"You shall speak in the same pulpit where I will give my speech," said Brutus.

"I desire no more," said Antony.

As soon as Brutus and the men left the room, Antony fell to Caesar's side and grabbed his arm. He pressed Caesar's hand to his face. He wept like a child.

"O pardon me that I am meek and gentle in front of these butchers," said Antony. "I prophesy a curse on the men who did this!"

A servant then entered the room. Antony recognized him as Octavius' servant. Octavius was Caesar's nephew. He started to tell Antony that Caesar had asked his master to come to Rome. Then he saw the bleeding body.

"Oh, Caesar!" cried the servant.

"Ride back and tell your master what has happened," commanded Antony. "But wait until after the funeral. Then you can report how the people have reacted to Caesar's cruel death."

Antony asked the young servant to help him with the body of his beloved friend. Together the men carried the bleeding body of mighty Caesar to the marketplace.

Act III
Scene 2

Brutus and Cassius made their way into the Forum. The crowd that awaited them was wild with anger. They screamed their protests. It took some time for Brutus to calm the mob. Finally they were persuaded to listen.

Brutus explained that he had loved Caesar as they had. He insisted he did not kill Caesar because he loved him less. He killed Caesar because he loved Rome more. Brutus told them that they would all be slaves if Caesar had lived. With Caesar's death, men could now live freely again.

"As Caesar loved me, I weep for him," said Brutus. "As he was valiant, I honor him. But as he was ambitious, I slew him." And Brutus added, "There are tears for his love, joy for his fortune, honor for his valor and death for his ambition."

The crowd had swiftly moved from Caesar's corner to that of Brutus. Now they cried out in support of Brutus.

"Here comes the body of Caesar mourned by Mark Antony, who had no hand in his death." Brutus explained. "I slew my best friend for the good of Rome. I have the same dagger for myself when it shall please my country to need my death." Antony and the servant put Caesar's body to rest on the steps. He watched Brutus, but his face showed no emotion.

The people cried, "Live, Brutus, live!!" They had

been won over. There were shouts that Brutus should be the new Caesar. They spoke of crowning him.

"Good countrymen, let me depart alone," said Brutus. "Stay here for Antony as he gives his speech about Caesar's glories. He is allowed to make this speech. I ask you not to depart until he has finished."

Brutus left and the crowd stayed on. The people agreed to hear Antony. They would obey Brutus' request. However, there were grumblings in the crowd. Some said that Caesar deserved his death. Others warned Antony not to speak against Brutus.

Antony walked to the top of the steps. He looked out at the crowd that had been Caesar's faithful. He wanted to shake with anger and accuse the guilty and their supporters. Instead he spoke calmly with carefully chosen words.

"Friends, Romans, countrymen, lend me your ears," said Antony. "I come to bury Caesar, not to praise him. The evil that men do lives after them. The good is often buried with their bones. So should it be with Caesar."

Standing alone on the steps, he looked down at the body of his friend. His loss was great and anger gripped him. But Antony spoke with calm resolve. He began by referring to Brutus as an honorable man. He reviewed Brutus' charges of Caesar's ambitions. Then he spoke of Caesar's loyalty to Rome. He said that when the poor had wept, Caesar had cried. He reminded them that Caesar had refused the crown when it had been offered to him three times. He talked about how the crowd had loved Caesar so that now they must mourn him. Antony reminded them again and again that he was not denying anything that Brutus had said.

Slowly the crowd began to read between the lines. They began to be swayed by Antony's words. They began to speak of a great wrong against Caesar. And they began to take pity on Antony whose eyes were red from weeping.

Then Antony produced a scroll. It was Caesar's will. He waved it high above the crowd.

"We'll hear the will," cried the crowd. "Read it, Mark Antony!"

Antony told them that he did not want to read it. It would prove how much Caesar had loved them.

"It will inflame you," said Antony. "It will make you mad."

"Read the will," shouted the people. "We'll hear it, Antony! You shall read us Caesar's will!"

Antony told the crowd to make a ring around him and the body. The people pressed forward. Antony wanted all to see the wounds that had caused the death. He described the wounds made by each conspirator. When he came to the final blow, he paused.

"For Brutus, as you know, was Caesar's angel. This was the unkindest cut of all," said Antony. "For when the noble Caesar saw him stab, his mighty heart burst."

The people began to shout for revenge. Antony quieted the crowd. He told them that he was not a good speaker like Brutus. All he did was to show them the wounds of Caesar. If he had been Brutus, he would have put a tongue in every wound so that the people would be moved to mutiny.

And, lo and behold, the crowd started to speak of mutiny.

"We'll mutiny," some cried.

"We'll burn the house of Brutus," shouted others.

Once again Antony calmed the crowd. He reminded them of the will he had yet to read.

"The will!" they cried. "Let's stay and hear the will!"

"Here is the will," said Antony. "To every Roman citizen he gives seventy-five drachmas. Moreover, he has left you all of his orchards. You may use these for public recreation. Here was a Caesar! When comes such another?"

The crowd went wild. They insisted on taking Caesar's body to burn it in a holy place. They would use the branches from the funeral pyre to burn down the traitors' houses. As the mourners left in a frenzy, Antony looked on approvingly. He had worked the crowd to his own purpose. And the results had been exactly what he planned.

As Antony thought about his next move, Octavius' servant appeared. He announced that his master had come to Rome. He was staying at Caesar's house. Antony was pleased. There could be no better time for Caesar's nephew to visit Rome!

The servant reported that Brutus and Cassius had ridden like madmen out of the city gates. Antony had moved the people to great anger. Now the traitors felt this anger like fire at their heels. Caesar's death would be avenged.

"Bring me to Octavius," said Antony. He vowed that this was only the beginning. These men would not go unpunished.

Act III
Scene 3

Cinna the poet was very unlucky to be walking the streets when he was met by an angry mob. The crowd began to question him. Who was he? Where did he live? Where was he going? Cinna explained that he was on his way to Caesar's funeral.

"As a friend or an enemy?" asked one of the Romans.

"As a friend," replied Cinna.

"What is your name?" demanded another.

"My name is Cinna," he replied.

The answer enraged the group. They had mistaken him to be one of the traitors.

"Tear him to pieces!" cried a voice in the crowd. "He is a conspirator."

"I am Cinna the poet!" insisted Cinna. He knew instantly that he was in grave danger.

"Tear him to pieces for his bad poetry," shouted one in the crowd.

"I am not Cinna the conspirator," said Cinna.

"It is no matter," said one in the crowd. "His name is Cinna, so he will die."

With that the crowd of Romans fell on him and beat him to death. Their anger was violent. The mission for revenge would face no obstacle. The wild men moved on through the streets dragging the body of the murdered poet.

"To Brutus', to Cassius', to Decius', to Casca's," cried

the crowd members. "Burn all!"

The people's fury had been churned to a feverish pitch. They could be satisfied by nothing but more bloodshed.

Act IV
Scene 1

Nearby in Antony's house, Octavius and Lepidus were meeting to discuss plans. They were making a list of men who must die. Octavius told Lepidus that his brother must be on this list. Lepidus agreed without resistance. Then he added the condition that Antony's nephew must also die.

"He shall not live," said Antony without emotion. "Look, with a spot I damn him," he added. And he put a large black spot of ink by his nephew's name.

Antony told Lepidus to go to Caesar's house and find his will. Antony wanted to change the will. He wanted Caesar's money to support their armies. He had little interest in the commoners' seventy-five drachmas now. When Lepidus left, Antony said that he was not worthy to share the rule of Rome. Octavius protested saying that Lepidus was a brave soldier.

"So is my horse," said Antony. He complained that Lepidus was a follower and not a leader. He criticized him for many reasons. But Octavius heard something different. From these complaints, he understood that Antony did not want to share power with two other men. He wanted to cut one of those men out. Octavius knew right then that Antony would also cut him out if he could. His intentions were clear.

Antony shifted the discussion to the need to raise an army to defeat Brutus and Cassius. But Octavius was no longer listening. He was really thinking about something else. He was thinking that Antony's grief over Caesar's death was short-lived. He wondered if Antony was actually pleased with the events that had unfolded.

Act IV

Scene 2

In the hills near Sardis, Brutus had set up camp with his army. He waited to hear from Cassius, but he was angry with his ally. He had sent word that he needed money for his army. Cassius had ignored this request, which left Brutus deeply insulted.

All day Brutus had thought about Cassius. How could he have been treated with such disrespect? It was unthinkable. A man of honor would surely have sent the funds immediately. Like an open wound, Cassius' rejection had festered. Now their friendship was infected.

Late in the afternoon, Pindarus, Cassius' servant, rode into camp. He announced that his master was on his way. Pindarus told Brutus that his master would set things right. But Brutus was too angry to believe him.

Minutes later Cassius arrived at the camp. As he dismounted his horse, Brutus frowned. Cassius knew he was angry.

"Most noble brother, you have done me wrong," said Cassius.

"If I don't wrong my enemies, it would be unlikely that I would wrong a brother!" said Brutus.

"Brutus, your sober manner hides the wrongs you do," shouted Cassius. His voice was suddenly very loud and angry.

Brutus told him to lower his voice. He suggested they discuss their differences in privacy. Both men told their commanders to lead their armies a distance away from the camp. They did not want the men to hear the argument that would soon take place. The guards at the door of the tent were told not to interrupt them.

Act IV
Scene 3

Once inside the tent, the anger was freed to run its course. Cassius was also angry with Brutus. Brutus had accused a friend of his of taking bribes. Brutus said that he should not have defended the man. And then Cassius told Brutus that he was wrong to criticize him at such a time as this. Brutus accused Cassius for his "itching palm," suggesting that he himself had taken bribes.

The argument escalated. Brutus and Cassius screamed and shouted. The aides at the door of the tent feared there would be blows. Angry words hissed through the tent like an evil wind. Brutus charged that the hands of those involved in the death of Caesar, "the foremost man of all this world," should not be involved with the taking of bribes. Cassius denied all. At every accusation, Cassius pled innocence. He tried in vain to defend himself. He told Brutus that he did not deny his request for money for the army. The messenger had made a mistake in answering this request. Finally Cassius accused Brutus of not loving him as a friend.

"I don't like your faults," said Brutus.

"A friendly eye would never see such faults," said Cassius. Then he pulled his dagger out of its sheath. He offered it to Brutus.

"Strike as you did to Caesar," said Cassius. "For I know, when you hated him worst, you loved him better than you loved Cassius."

Brutus began to feel sympathy for Cassius. He appeared to be so pitiful. There he was offering his dagger to end his own life. The heat of the argument began to cool.

"Put your dagger away," said Brutus. "I have been ill-tempered."

"Do you confess that?" asked Cassius. "Give me your hand."

"And my heart, too," said Brutus.

The men moved toward one another and shook hands. Cassius apologized for his temper, which he said he had inherited from his mother. Brutus also apologized. They regretted the things that they had said in anger. They needed to stand together.

"I have been sick from so much grief," said Brutus. Then he told Cassius about the death of his wife. Cassius was shocked that Portia was gone. She had seemed to be in such good health only a week ago.

"Oh, touching loss," said Cassius. "What illness caused her death?"

"She was in despair about my absence," said Brutus. "And she greatly worried about Antony's and Octavius' alliance. She became so upset that she killed herself by swallowing hot coals."

"Oh, immortal gods!" cried Cassius, who put his head in his hands.

"Speak of her no more," said Brutus. He called for a bowl of wine, and a servant entered with one. "In this I bury all unkindness," he said. Then he drank deeply from the bowl. He offered it to his friend.

"My heart is thirsty for that noble pledge," said Cassius.

As the sun slowly set behind the hills, the men sat in silence. By and by, Titinius and Messala, friends from

Rome, entered the tent. They announced that Octavius and Antony had brought their armies to Philippi. They also reported that arrest warrants for the execution of 100 senators had been issued.

The men discussed battle plans. Cassius felt that it would be better to wait for the attack. In this way, the opposing armies would be tired from the marching. Brutus wanted to march to Philippi. The villages along the way were not friendly to their cause. But if Antony and Octavius marched through the area, they would pick up many recruits. They would be given encouragement and refreshment along the way.

"But hear me, good brother," protested Cassius. He did not agree with Brutus' plan.

"Pardon me," interrupted Brutus, "our armies are ready. They are now the best that they can be. There is a tide in the affairs of men that taken at the flood can lead on to fortune. On such a full sea are we now afloat. And we must take the current or lose our ventures."

Brutus' words impressed Cassius. Perhaps Brutus was right after all. And he did not want to make his friend angry when they had just mended their rift.

"Then we will go to Philippi and meet them," agreed Cassius.

The men said good night to one another. Brutus then called his servant Lucius. He asked him to play his lute. He invited some of his closest men to come and sleep in the tent. The men, Varro and Claudius, did not want to lie down. They wanted to stand watch, but Brutus insisted.

As Lucius played his lute, Brutus read from a small book that he found in his robe. He was grateful for the soothing sound of the music. Unfortunately, the boy was very tired and quickly nodded off.

Brutus carefully took the instrument from the

sleeping boy's arms. He didn't want it to fall and break. He then returned to his book, looking for the last page he had read. Above his book, a shadow in the corner caught his eye. He looked up to see what it was. It appeared to be a misty shape of a person. Brutus strained his eyes to see better. It could not be what he thought it was. Surely this was not true! It appeared to be the ghost of Caesar.

"Speak to me," demanded Brutus. "Who are you?"

"Thy evil spirit, Brutus," answered the ghostly presence.

"Why are you here?" asked Brutus.

"To tell thee thou shall see me at Phillipi," said the ghost.

With that the ghost disappeared. Brutus shook off his astonishment. He woke Lucius, Varro and Claudius, asking each if they had cried out in their sleep. Brutus searched for some explanation of his vision. There was none. Finally, he concluded that Caesar's ghost had really visited him.

He told Claudius to go tell Cassius that they would move the armies very early in the morning. He was ready to meet his fate, whatever that might be.

Act V
Scene 1

At Philippi, Octavius and Antony waited with their armies. The air was heavy with anticipation. Finally a messenger arrived to warn them. The enemy was now approaching. Antony ordered Octavius to charge from the left. He would cover the right side of the battlefield. Octavius objected. He insisted that he would cover the right.

"Why do you cross me?" asked Antony. He was irritated that Octavius would not follow his orders.

"I'll do as I see fit," answered Octavius. Although he admired Antony, he saw no reason why he should take orders from him. After all, he was the true heir to Caesar's throne.

Brutus and Cassius rode to Antony and Octavius. They wanted to meet with them one last time before the battle started.

"Words before blows," said Brutus. "Is it not so, countrymen?"

"Not that we love words better, as you do," answered Octavius.

"Good words are better than bad strokes, Octavius" said Brutus.

"In your bad strokes, Brutus, you give good words," said Antony. "Witness the hole you made in Caesar's heart as you cried, 'Long live Caesar!'"

And so it continued in the last minutes prior to battle. The men traded insults until Octavius and

Antony rode away. As they left, they taunted Brutus and Cassius to fight if they had the stomachs for the battle.

This brief meeting sobered Brutus and Cassius. They both realized that they could be nearing the end. They rode slowly back. At camp, Cassius told Messala that today was his birthday. Then he grabbed his hand and told him that he should be his witness. He declared that he did not want to risk all of Rome's liberties on this one battle. He didn't have a good feeling about the battle today. Messala tried to reassure him that everything would end well.

Cassius then turned to Brutus. He told him that he hoped they would win the battle today. But he added that they should be prepared for the worst.

"If we do lose this battle, then this is the last time we shall speak together," said Cassius. "If we lose, what will you do?"

Brutus told Cassius that he thought it would be cowardly if he killed himself. Cassius was surprised.

"Are you contented to be led through the streets of Rome?" asked Cassius.

"No, Cassius, I will not," said Brutus. "This day must end the work that began on the ides of March. If we do meet again, we shall smile. If not, we have said our farewells."

"Forever and ever, farewell," said Cassius.

Act V
Scene 2

Brutus and Messala looked out at the battlefield. Brutus was determining the strategy that should be used. He carefully looked at the left flank and then to the right. It appeared to him that there was a weakness in Octavius' army.

"Tell the men to attack immediately," said Brutus. "Octavius' men seem to be lacking in courage. A sudden push from our forces may well overthrow them."

Messala rode off immediately to follow Brutus' orders. He did not think that the right flank of Octavius' troops looked weak, but he would never question the noble Brutus. He would follow the orders carefully and hope for the best.

Brutus watched Messala ride off. He too hoped for the best. Yet, he could not stop thinking about the ghost of Caesar that had visited him last night. Would he actually see Caesar on the battlefield today? He shuddered to consider the possibility.

Act V

Scene 3

Cassius and Titinius watched the fighting from another area of the battlefield. Cassius saw that his men were retreating. He was so furious that he killed his own flag bearer for turning back. Brutus had charged Octavius' army too soon. His soldiers started looting instead of protecting Cassius' forces. This had given Antony the opportunity to encircle Cassius' army.

Pindarus, Cassius' servant, arrived to warn Cassius that Antony was in the camp. Cassius strained to see his camp.

"The hill is far away," said Cassius. "Are those my tents on fire?"

"They are my lord," said Titinius.

"Ride my horse as fast as you can," said Cassius. "I must know if the troops in my camp are friends or enemy."

Titinius agreed to do this as soon as possible. Then Cassius asked Pindarus to climb a high hill. He was ordered to report the situation on the battlefield. When Pindarus left, Cassius prepared to die.

"This is the day that I drew my first breath," he said. "Time has come full circle. My life has run its compass."

"Oh, my lord!" cried Pindarus from the hill.

"What news?" asked Cassius.

"Titinius is surrounded yet he spurs on," reported

Pindarus. "Oh, he has been captured!"

In the distance there were shouts from the army. The report must be correct. Cassius was resigned. The time had come.

"Come down, Pindarus," cried Cassius. "What a coward I am to see my best friend taken by the enemy."

Pindarus climbed down from the hill. He stood before his master. Cassius reminded him of the day they had met. He had saved his life. Pindarus promised that he would always do whatever Cassius requested. Today Cassius asked Pindarus to take the sword that Cassius had used to kill Caesar and kill him. Pindarus refused. But Cassius insisted. Finally, Pindarus took the sword that Cassius pushed toward him. He thrust it into his master's heart. As Cassius fell to the ground, Pindarus was overcome with grief.

"So I am set free," he cried. "Yet it is against my will. Oh, Cassius! I will run away from this country. No Roman will ever find me."

Pindarus took a final farewell look at his kind master and turned. On the heels of his departure, Messala and Titinius entered camp. They were discussing the battle. Octavius had been defeated by Brutus. But Cassius' army was defeated by Antony's. They wanted to share the news with Cassius. Where was he? Suddenly they saw his body on the ground.

"He looks like he is dead," said Titinius.

"Oh, he did not have any hope of success," said Messala. "That is why he became depressed. We must break the news to Brutus." He left.

Titinius knelt. "Cassius, didn't you see that I was given this wreath of victory?" he demanded of the lifeless body of his friend. "Did you not hear the shouts? Did you misunderstand everything?"

He placed the victory garland on Cassius' head.

Brutus had asked that it be given to him. Titinius picked up Cassius' sword and held it to his chest.

"This is a Roman's part," he said. "Come Cassius' sword and find Titinius' heart." With those words, he thrust the dagger into his chest. His body fell and slumped next to his commander.

Meanwhile, Messala had told Brutus about Cassius' death. He led Brutus and some his officers to the place where Cassius lay. They were horrified to find Titinius' bleeding body next to his.

"Oh, Julius Caesar, thou art mighty yet," cried Brutus. "Your spirit walks among us, turning our swords into our bowels."

"Look how Titinius crowned Cassius," said Young Cato, pointing to the victory laurel on his head.

"Friends, I owe more tears to this dead man than I can pay," said Brutus mournfully. He told his officers to take the body away. A funeral ceremony must be held later. All others returned to the battlefield.

Act V
Scene 4

B rutus and his men fought valiantly against the forces of Antony and Octavius. Even though the tide was turning against them, they never gave up.

Young Cato was killed. Lucilius found himself cornered by enemy troops. He decided to tell them that he was Brutus. If they killed him, then Brutus' life could be spared.

"I am Brutus," shouted Lucilius.

"Surrender or die!" shouted one of Antony's soldiers as he held his sword at Lucilius' throat.

"Kill Brutus and be honored by his death," said Lucilius. He handed over his purse as a bribe.

"We must not. You are a noble prisoner," said the soldier.

Just then Antony came upon the scene. The soldier told him that Brutus had been taken, which of course was not true.

"Where is he?" asked Antony.

"Safe, Antony. Brutus is safe. No enemy shall ever take the noble Brutus," said Lucilius. "The gods will protect him from so great a shame."

"This is not Brutus," said Antony. "But he is a prize worth keeping. Keep this man safe and treat him well. I would rather have such men as my friends than enemies."

Then he instructed his men to find out whether Brutus was alive or dead.

Act V

Scene 5

Nearby, Brutus and his men were resting on a large rock under a shady tree. The men were all weary of fighting. Morale was low. Everyone knew that the outcome was unlikely to be favorable. Their scout had not returned to camp. He had probably been killed or captured.

Brutus leaned toward his officer Clitus. He whispered something in his ear. Clitus fell back as if something had burned him.

"What, I, my lord?" said Clitus. "Not for all the world. I'd rather kill myself."

Next Brutus whispered into Dardanius' ear. A look of horror crossed his face.

"Shall I do such a deed?" he said. Brutus had proposed the unthinkable.

Brutus walked away from the shady spot where the men were resting.

"What terrible request did Brutus ask of you?" asked Clitus.

"To kill him," answered Dardanius.

"His grief is overflowing," said Clitus.

Both men watched their noble leader as he stared at nothing. He called out to Volumnius, who joined him. Brutus put his arm around the man's shoulders.

"Volumnius, the ghost of Caesar has appeared to me," said Brutus. "I know my hour has come."

"Not so, my lord," protested Volumnius.

"Yes, our enemies have beat us," said Brutus. "It is better if we leap into the grave than wait until they push us. We have been friends since we two went to school together. For our friendship, I beg you to hold my sword while I run into it."

"That is no duty for a friend, my lord," said Volumnius.

In the background the sounds of battle were becoming louder. Brutus and Volumnius both knew what would happen soon. Clitus ran over to them and told them they must flee. The enemy troops were approaching. Brutus shook hands with his men and said farewell.

"My life is almost over," said Brutus. "Night hangs upon my eyes. My bones are weary."

The men begged Brutus to leave with them. He promised that he would follow shortly. Strato stayed behind to wait with him.

"Strato, please stay with me," said Brutus. "You have led an honorable life. Turn your face. Hold your sword while I run into it."

Strato looked at the enemy approaching. He then looked into the eyes of the honorable Brutus. He would help this man choose his own death.

"Give me your hand first," said Strato.

Brutus clutched his hand tightly.

"Farewell, good Strato," said Brutus. "Caesar, now be still." Brutus pushed forward with a great force. He thrust his body against the blade and fell into his friend's arms. Strato put his arms around Brutus. He gently put his body to rest on the ground.

Antony, Octavius, and Messala came upon the clearing as Strato was leaving.

"Where is your master?" Messala asked Strato.

"Free from the bondage you are in, Messala," said Strato. "The conquerors can only make a fire of him. He defeated himself."

The men gathered around Brutus' body.

"This was the noblest Roman of them all," said Antony. "All of the conspirators except he did what they did out of envy of great Caesar. He was the only one who thought of the good of the common man. His life was gentle. Nature might stand up and say to all the world, 'This was a man!'"

"Let us give him all the respect and rites of burial," said Octavius. "Tonight his bones will lie in my tent, as we would honor a true soldier."

And so the men of Octavius' and Antony's armies were victorious in avenging Caesar's death. The victory celebration was subdued. There had been much blood shed that day. The price of revenge was great.

JULIUS CAESAR

THE PLAY

Cast of Characters

JULIUS CAESAR

Triumvirs after the death of Julius Caesar:
OCTAVIUS CAESAR
MARK ANTONY (called Antony or Antonio)
M. AEMILIUS LEPIDUS (called Lepidus)

Senators:
CICERO
PUBLIUS
POPILIUS LENA

Conspirators against Julius Caesar:
MARCUS BRUTUS (called Brutus)
CASSIUS
CASCA
TREBONIUS
CAIUS LIGARIUS (called Ligarius)
DECIUS BRUTUS
METELLUS CIMBER
CINNA

FLAVIUS AND MARULLUS, *tribunes of the people*
ARTEMIDORUS, *a teacher of rhetoric*
A SOOTHSAYER
CINNA, *a poet*

Friends to Brutus and Cassius:
LUCILIUS
TITINIUS
MESSALA
YOUNG CATO
VOLUMNIUS

Servants to Brutus:
VARRO
CLITUS
CLAUDIUS
STRATO
LUCIUS
DARDANIUS

Servants, citizens (plebians), guards, attendants, carpenter, cobbler, the army (soldiers)

PINDARUS, *servant to Cassius*
CALPURNIA, *wife to Caesar*
PORTIA, *wife to Brutus*
THE GHOST OF CAESAR

Act I
Scene 1

Setting: A street in Rome.

(Flavius, Marullus, and a group of Commoners enter the stage.)

FLAVIUS: You idle creatures, get you home! Is this a holiday? Don't you know you should be wearing your work clothes? What is your trade?

CARPENTER: Why, sir, a carpenter.

MARULLUS: Where is your leather apron and ruler? Why are you wearing your best clothes? And what is your trade, sir?

COBBLER: Truly, sir, I am a cobbler.

MARULLUS: But what is your trade? Tell me plainly!

COBBLER: I am a mender of bad soles.

FLAVIUS: Why aren't you in your shop today? Why do you lead these men in the streets?

COBBLER: Truly, sir, to wear out their shoes, to get myself more work. Sir, we are taking a holiday to see Caesar and to rejoice in his triumph.

MARULLUS: Why rejoice? What conquests does he bring home? You blocks, you stones, you worse than senseless things! Oh, you hard hearts!

Don't you remember Pompey? Many times you climbed to the top of the walls and towers. Patiently you waited to see the great Pompey. As soon as his chariot appeared, the crowd raised such a shout that the Tiber River shook from the echoes. And now you put on your best clothes and make a holiday? To throw flowers on the paths for Caesar, who comes in triumph over Pompey's blood? Be gone! Go home! Fall on your knees. Pray to the gods that they don't send a plague for your ingratitude.

FLAVIUS: Go, go, good countrymen. Go down to the Tiber River banks. There fill the river with your tears till the water comes up to the top of the highest shore.

(The commoners exit.)

See how they vanish, tongue-tied because of their guilt. You go toward the Capitol and I'll go this way. We will take the decorations off the statues we pass on our way.

MARULLUS: Can we do it? You know it is the feast of Lupercal.

FLAVIUS: It doesn't matter. Let no statues be hung with Caesar's trophies. We will also drive the crowds home where we see them gathered. We need to keep Caesar in his place, as a man. Else he would soar above us, keeping us as fearful servants.

(They exit.)

Act I

Scene 2

Setting: A street in Rome.

(Caesar, Antony, Calpurnia, Portia, Decius, Cicero, Brutus, Cassius, Casca, a large crowd including a soothsayer; after all, Marullus and Flavius.) (Music plays.)

CAESAR: Calpurnia.

CASCA: Quiet! Caesar speaks. *(Music stops.)*

CAESAR: Calpurnia.

CALPURNIA: Here I am, my lord.

CAESAR: Stand directly in Antonio's way when he runs his course. Antonio!

ANTONY: Caesar, my lord?

CAESAR: Don't forget to touch Calpurnia when you run. Our elders say that women who are barren will shake off the sterile curse if touched by a runner in this race.

ANTONY: I shall remember. When Caesar says, 'do this,' it is done.

SOOTHSAYER: Caesar!

CAESAR: Who calls?

CASCA: Quiet! *(Music ceases again.)*

CAESAR: Who is it in this crowd that calls my name?

I hear a voice shriller than the music cry, 'Caesar!' Speak. I am turned to hear.

SOOTHSAYER: Beware the ides of March.

CAESAR: Who is that man?

BRUTUS: A soothsayer tells you to beware of the ides of March.

CAESAR: Bring him before me. Let me see his face.

CASSIUS: Fellow, come out of the crowd. Look at Caesar.

CAESAR: What do you say to me now? Speak again.

SOOTHSAYER: Beware the ides of March.

CAESAR: He is a dreamer. Let us leave him.

(All exit except Brutus and Cassius.)

CASSIUS: Are you going to watch the running?

BRUTUS: No.

CASSIUS: Brutus, I have noticed lately that you are not as kind to me as you used to be. You are cold to me, your friend, who loves you.

BRUTUS: Cassius, if I have appeared cold, don't think that I am not your true friend. I have been thinking of private matters. It is my problem. I am at war with myself. So, I forget to show my love for my fellow man.

CASSIUS: Then I was mistaken. Tell me, can you see your own face?

BRUTUS: No, for the eye sees not itself, but by reflection.

CASSIUS: Of course. It is very sad, Brutus, that you don't have an inside mirror to see your inner worth. I have heard some of the best men in Rome (except Caesar), talking about you. They were groaning under the weight of Caesar's rule. They wished that you, Brutus, had his eyes.

BRUTUS: Would you lead me into danger, Cassius? Are you asking me to look for something that is not in me?

CASSIUS: Since you can't see yourself, I will be your mirror. I will show your qualities, which you are too modest to see. Don't be suspicious of me, Brutus. You know I am not a flatterer.

(Shouting offstage.)

BRUTUS: What is that shouting for? I do fear the people choose Caesar for their king.

CASSIUS: Do you fear it? Then I think you would not have it so.

BRUTUS: I would not, Cassius. Yet I love him well. But why do you keep me here? What is it you want to tell me? If your purpose is for the welfare of Rome, tell me. For I see honor and death both the same. I love honor more than I fear death.

CASSIUS: I know that honor is a virtue in you, Brutus. Honor is the subject of my story. I don't know how you and other men see life. But as for me, I'd rather not live than live like this. That is, to treat a mere man as a god. I was born as free as Caesar, and so were you. Am I a wretched creature who must bend if Caesar nods?

(Shouting offstage.)

BRUTUS: Another shout? I think this applause is for

some new honors heaped on Caesar.

CASSIUS: Why does Caesar walk the world like a Colossus, and we petty men walk under his huge legs? Men are masters of their fates. The fault is not in the stars, but in ourselves. When in the history of the world has one man alone held such power in Rome?

BRUTUS: I have thought about this. But for now, I would ask you to speak of it no more. I will choose a time in the future to hear more about what you have said. Till then, think of this. Brutus would rather be a poor villager than a son of Rome under these hard times.

CASSIUS: I am glad that my weak words have struck a show of fire from Brutus.

(Caesar and his followers enter.)

BRUTUS: The games are done. Caesar is returning.

CASSIUS: As they pass, ask Casca what happened.

BRUTUS: I will. But look, Cassius, how there's an angry spot on Caesar's brow. And all the rest look like punished children. Calpurnia is pale. Cicero looks as angry as he does when he argues with senators at the Capitol.

CAESAR: Antonio, let me have men about me that are fat. That Cassius has a lean and hungry look. He thinks too much. Such men are dangerous.

ANTONY: Fear him not. He's not dangerous. He is a noble Roman.

74

CAESAR:	I am not afraid of him. If I were capable of fear, I would avoid Cassius. He reads much. He is a great watcher. He looks through a man. He doesn't like plays, as you do, Antony. He doesn't listen to music. He seldom smiles. Men like him are never relaxed, especially around greater men. Thus, they are very dangerous. I am not telling you what I fear, but what there is to fear. For I am Caesar.
	(Caesar and his followers exit.)
CASCA:	Did you want to speak with me?
BRUTUS:	Yes, Casca. Tell us what happened today that Caesar looks so sad.
CASCA:	Why, the crown was offered to him. He pushed it away with his hand. The crowd shouted.
BRUTUS:	What was the second noise for?
CASCA:	Why, for that too.
CASSIUS:	They shouted three times. What was the last cry for?
CASCA:	Why, for that too.
BRUTUS:	Was the crown offered to him three times?
CASCA:	Yes, and he pushed it away three times. But in my mind, each time he pushed it away more gently. And every time he pushed it away, the crowd shouted.
CASSIUS:	Who offered him the crown?
CASCA:	Why, Antony. And then Caesar fainted. He fell down in the market place. He foamed at the mouth and was speechless.

BRUTUS:	It is likely that he has the falling sickness. What did he say when he came to?
CASCA:	Well, before he fell down, he noticed the crowd was pleased when he refused the crown. So, he opened his cloak and offered to cut his throat. I would have done it for him. Then he came to again. He said if he had done anything wrong, it was because of his sickness. Three or four women near me cried. They said, 'Alas, good soul,' and forgave him with all their hearts. But pay no attention to them. If Caesar had stabbed their own mothers they would have forgiven him.
BRUTUS:	And after that, he came away sad?
CASCA:	Ay.
CASSIUS:	Did Cicero say anything?
CASCA:	Ay. He spoke Greek.
CASSIUS:	What did he say?
CASCA:	I have no idea. Those that understood him smiled at one another and shook their heads. But it was Greek to me. I'll tell you more news. Marullus and Flavius, for pulling scarves off Caesar's statues, were executed.
CASSIUS:	Will you join me for supper tonight?
CASCA:	No, I am promised elsewhere.
CASSIUS:	Will you dine with me tomorrow?
CASCA:	Ay. If I am alive, and you don't change your mind. And if your dinner is worth eating.
CASSIUS:	Good. I will expect you then.

CASCA:	Do so then. Farewell to both of you. *(Exits.)*
BRUTUS:	What a blunt fellow. He used to be lively when we were in school together.
CASSIUS:	He is still lively in actions. When he speaks, he pretends to be slow on purpose. It makes him more believable.
BRUTUS:	That appears so. I leave you now. Tomorrow, if you wish to speak with me, I will come to your home. Or you can come to my home.
CASSIUS:	I will. Till then, think of the world.

(Brutus exits.)

Well, Brutus! Even though you are honorable, I see you are open to change. It is right that we work together. After all, who is so set in his ways that he cannot be persuaded? Caesar doesn't like me, but he loves Brutus. If I were Brutus, I wouldn't listen to me. Tonight, I will write some notes using different handwriting on each. I will throw them through Brutus' window. It will look like different citizens are praising Brutus and criticizing Caesar. After that, Caesar's ambition will be checked. He will be shaken from his seat of power, or worse.

Act I
Scene 3

Setting: A street in Rome.

(Thunder and lightning. Casca enters with his sword drawn. Cicero enters from the opposite side of the stage.)

CICERO: Good evening, Casca. Why are you breathless?

CASCA: Aren't you trembling when all the world seems to be shaking? I have seen great storms on land and sea! But never have I seen a fire from heaven as I have seen tonight. There must be a civil war above.

CICERO: What have you seen?

CASCA: I saw a well-known slave. He held up his hand, which became a torch. Yet his hand remained unburned. After that I saw a lion by the Capitol. It just stared at me and let me pass by. Then a hundred terrified women swore they saw men on fire walking up and down the streets. Yesterday the night bird sat in the marketplace at noon and hooted and shrieked. Don't tell me there's a good explanation. I believe these things are a sign that something is about to happen.

CICERO:	It is indeed a strange time. But different men will decide on different reasons for these events. Does Caesar come to the Capitol tomorrow?
CASCA:	He does. He told Antony to send word to you that he would be there tomorrow.
CICERO:	Good night, then. We should not be walking under this disturbed sky.
CASCA:	Farewell, Cicero.

(Cicero exits. Cassius enters.)

CASSIUS:	Who's there?
CASCA:	A Roman.
CASSIUS:	Casca, by your voice.
CASCA:	You hear well. Cassius, what night is this?
CASSIUS:	A very pleasing night to honest men.
CASCA:	Whoever knew the heavens could be so menacing?
CASSIUS:	Those who have seen many bad things on earth. As for me, I have been walking the streets with my cloak opened. I have bared my chest to the thunderbolt. I stood in the path of the blue lightning.
CASCA:	Why did you tempt the heavens so? It is man's nature to fear the gods when they send us signs to astonish us.
CASSIUS:	If you were a true Roman, you would not be afraid to see the storm. The lion in the Capitol is like this man who has grown as big and fearful as these storms.
CASCA:	'Tis Caesar that you mean, is it not, Cassius?

79

CASSIUS: Let it be who it is. For now Romans are governed by their mothers' womanish ways.

CASCA: Indeed, they say tomorrow the senators mean to establish Caesar as a king.

CASSIUS: I know where I will wear this dagger then. I will kill myself. Nothing can make me live life under a tyrant. I can always choose death instead.

CASCA: So can I. Every man has the power to end his captivity.

CASSIUS: Why should Caesar be a tyrant then? He wouldn't be such a wolf if Romans weren't such sheep. What am I saying? You may be a willing servant of Caesar's. If you are, I have weapons and I am not afraid.

CASCA: You speak to Casca, and I am not a telltale. If you mount a rebellion, I will be with you.

(They shake hands.)

CASSIUS: I have already persuaded some of the best Romans to follow me. I have an honorable but dangerous plan. These men wait for me now at Pompey's porch. This is no night for walking in the streets.

(Cinna enters.)

CASCA: Stay close by here. Here comes someone in haste.

CASSIUS: 'Tis Cinna. He is a friend.

CINNA: Who's with you?

CASSIUS: Casca. He's with us in our plan.

CINNA: Oh, Cassius. If only you could win the noble Brutus to our cause.

CASSIUS:	Be content. Good Cinna, take these notes, and put them in Brutus' house where he will see them. When you finish, go to Pompey's Theater, where you shall find us. Are Decius Brutus and Trebonius there?
CINNA:	All but Metellus Cimber. He's gone to look for you at your house. Well, I will go. I will leave these notes as you told me.
CASSIUS:	Come, Casca, you and I will see Brutus at his house. He is three quarters ours. The next meeting will win him over.
CASCA:	He sits high in the people's hearts. That which is offensive in us can be changed to virtue and worthiness by Brutus.
CASSIUS:	Our great need of him is as you say. Let us go. It is after midnight. And before daylight we must wake him and get him on our side.

Act II
Scene 1

Setting: Brutus' home.

(Brutus enters his orchard.)

BRUTUS: What time is it, Lucius? I can't tell by looking at the stars. Wake up, Lucius.

(Lucius enters.)

LUCIUS: You called me, my lord?

BRUTUS: Light a candle and bring it to me.

LUCIUS: I will, my lord. *(Exits.)*

BRUTUS: He must be killed. I have no bad feelings against him. But for the good of the people, he must go. He wants to be crowned. A crown would make him too dangerous.

Truthfully, I have never known Caesar to misuse power. But it could happen. When the climber gets to the top of the ladder, he turns his back on those below. Caesar might be the same. We should think of him as a snake's egg and kill him in the shell before he is hatched.

(Lucius enters.)

LUCIUS: I lit the candle in your room. While I was looking for the flint, I found this note. It was not there when I went to bed.

(Gives him the letter.)

BRUTUS: Go back to bed. It is not day. Is tomorrow the ides of March?

LUCIUS: I know not, sir.

BRUTUS: Look at the calendar and tell me.

LUCIUS: I will, sir.

(Exits.)

BRUTUS: The meteors shooting through the air give so much light that I can read by them.

(Opens the letter and reads aloud.)

'Brutus, you sleep. Awake and see yourself. Shall Rome . . . . .?' I have to figure this out. 'Speak, strike, redress! Brutus, you sleep. Awake.'

What does it mean? Oh, Rome! I promise thee. If there are wrongs, Brutus is the man to right them.

(Lucius enters.)

LUCIUS: Sir, March is fifteen days gone.

(Knocking sound is heard offstage.)

BRUTUS: 'Tis good. Go to the gate. Someone knocks.

(Lucius exits.)

I have not slept since Cassius first turned me against Caesar. It feels like I am in a hideous dream. The time between planning an act and doing an act is awful.

(Lucius enters.)

LUCIUS: Sir, 'tis your brother-in-law, Cassius, at the door.

BRUTUS: Is he alone?

LUCIUS: No, there are more with him.

BRUTUS: Do you know any of them?

LUCIUS: No, sir. Their hats are covering half their faces. Their cloaks are covering the other half. So I cannot tell who they are.

BRUTUS: Let them enter.

(Lucius exits.)

Those are the men. Oh, conspiracy! Are you ashamed to show your face even in the darkest hour of night? Don't try to hide yourselves. Rather, hide your plans behind smiles.

(The conspirators enter: Cassius, Casca, Decius Brutus, Cinna, Metellus Cimber, and Trebonius.)

CASSIUS: I think we are intruding on your rest. Good morning, Brutus. Are we bothering you?

BRUTUS: I have been up all night long. Do I know these men with you ?

CASSIUS: Yes, every one of them. Every man here honors you. This is Trebonius, Decius Brutus, Casca, Cinna, Metellus Cimber.

BRUTUS: They are all welcome here.

CASSIUS: May I have a word?

(Brutus and Cassius whisper and then return to the group)

BRUTUS: Give me your hands, one by one.

CASSIUS: And let us swear our resolution.

BRUTUS: No, not an oath. If any man is so weak that

he needs to swear an oath, then he should drop out now. We don't need an oath to do what we are bound to do. People swear an oath when they are afraid that they may be too cowardly to go through with a plan. We are Romans and our honor is enough.

CASSIUS: What about Cicero? Shall we see if he wants to join us? I think he would stand very strong with us.

CASCA: Let us not leave him out.

CINNA: No, he should be included.

METELLUS: Yes. He is old and respected. That will give our cause strength. With him on our side, people won't say our deeds were wild because of our youth.

BRUTUS: No. Leave him out. He never follows any plan that he didn't think of himself.

CASSIUS: Then leave him out.

CASCA: Indeed, he is not fit.

DECIUS: Is Caesar the only one to be touched?

CASSIUS: That is a good question, Decius. I don't think his beloved Mark Antony should outlive Caesar. He will definitely cause us trouble afterwards. Let Antony and Caesar fall together.

BRUTUS: Our course would seem too bloody. To cut off the head and then hack off the limbs is too much. Caesar is the head. Antony is but a limb of Caesar. Let us be sacrificers but not butchers. As for Mark Antony, don't worry about him.

CASSIUS: Yet, I fear him because of the love he bears to Caesar.

BRUTUS: Do not think of him, good Cassius. If he loves Caesar, all he can do is to die for Caesar. And that is unlikely as he is given to sports, wildness, and women.

TREBONIUS: There's nothing to worry about Antony. Let him live and he will laugh at this some day.

(The clock strikes.)

BRUTUS: Quiet. The clock strikes three.

TREBONIUS: 'Tis time to depart.

CASSIUS: There is doubt Caesar will come out today. He has been very superstitious lately. Maybe some of these omens will persuade him not to go to the Capitol today.

DECIUS: Don't worry. If he thinks like that, I can persuade him to go. I will go to his house to bring him to the Capitol.

CASSIUS: We will all be there to fetch him.

BRUTUS: By eight o'clock at the latest?

CINNA: That's the latest. Don't fail to be there.

METELLUS: Caius Ligarius hates Caesar. He berated him for speaking well of Pompey. I wonder why no one thought of him.

BRUTUS: Metellus, go get him. He loves me, and for good reason. I will talk him into our plan.

CASSIUS: It's getting late. Remember what you have said. Show yourselves as true Romans.

BRUTUS: Men, look fresh and merry. Don't let your faces spoil our plan. Do as our Roman actors do. Play your parts.

(All exit but Brutus.)

Boy! Lucius! Fast asleep? No matter. You are young. Enjoy your sleep. You are not bothered by the heavy cares of men. So you can sleep soundly.

(Portia enters.)

PORTIA: Brutus, my lord.

BRUTUS: Portia! Why are you up at this hour? It's not good for you in your weak condition to be out in the early morning cold air.

PORTIA: It's not good for your health either. Last night you left bed. Yesterday at supper you suddenly got up and started sighing. When I asked what was wrong, you gave me an unkind look. When I asked again, you angrily dismissed me from the room. Dear lord, make me acquainted with your cause of grief.

BRUTUS: I am not well. That is all.

PORTIA: If you were not well, you are wise enough to seek a cure.

BRUTUS: Why, so I do. Good Portia, go to bed.

PORTIA: If you were sick, you would not leave your bed in the middle of the night. No, you are not sick. There's something bothering your mind.

(Kneels.)

On my knees, I am begging you to tell me. I rely on my former beauty and our marriage vow to persuade you. I am your other half.

	Tell me why there were six or seven men here tonight. Why did they hide their faces even in the darkness?
BRUTUS:	(*Raises her.*) Kneel not, gentle Portia.
PORTIA:	I should not need to if you were gentle, Brutus. Am I only here to keep you company during meals? To comfort your bed? And to talk to you sometimes? If it be no more, I am not your wife.
BRUTUS:	You are my true and honorable wife. You are as dear to me as my heart's blood.
PORTIA:	If that were true then I would know the secret. I know I am only a woman. But I am a woman that married Brutus. I am the woman that was daughter to Cato. If you don't think I am strong enough to know the secret, I will prove it. Here, I gave myself this wound on the thigh. If I can bear that wound, I can keep my husband's secrets.
BRUTUS:	Oh, God! Render me worthy of this noble wife!
	(*Knocking heard.*) Someone is knocking. Go inside and I will tell you my secrets in awhile. I will share everything in my heart.
	(*Exit Portia. Enter Lucius and Caius Ligarius.*)
LUCIUS:	Here is a sick man who wants to speak with you.
BRUTUS:	Caius Ligarius, how are you?
CAIUS:	Greetings from a sick man.
BRUTUS:	What a time you picked to be sick.

CAIUS:	I am not sick if you are planning something honorable.
BRUTUS:	I would tell you of my honorable plan, if you were well.
CAIUS:	By all the gods of Rome, I hereby discard my sickness.
	(Throws off his neck kerchief.)
	Just tell me what to do and I will do it.
BRUTUS:	A piece of work that will make sick men well.
CAIUS:	But, don't we have to make a well man sick to do that?
BRUTUS:	That we must. Come. I will tell you our plan on the way.
CAIUS:	Lead the way. With a heart newly fired I follow you. To do what I know not. But it is sufficient that Brutus leads me on.
BRUTUS:	Follow me, then.
	(They exit.)

Act II

Scene 2

Thunder and lightning. Enter Julius Caesar, in his nightgown.

CAESAR: Neither heaven nor earth have been at peace tonight. Three times Calpurnia cried out in her sleep: 'Help! They murder Caesar!' Who's there?

(Enter Servant.)

SERVANT: My lord ?

CAESAR: Go to the priests. Find out what predictions they have for me today.

SERVANT: I will, my lord.

(Enter Calpurnia.)

CALPURNIA: What do you mean? Do you think you're going out today? You will not stir out of your house today.

CAESAR: I will go out. My fears will disappear when I face them.

CALPURNIA: Caesar, I never paid attention to omens. Now they frighten me. Besides my inner fear, I have heard from others. Graves have opened up and sent out their dead. An army of warriors fought a battle in the sky and dripped blood on the Capitol. Ghosts shrieked in the streets. These things are not normal and I fear them.

CAESAR: Who can avoid what the gods have planned? I will go forth. The strange things you described apply to everyone. So I have nothing to fear for myself.

CALPURNIA: These signs do not apply to everyone. When beggars die, there are no comets seen. When a prince dies, the heavens blaze with strange sights.

CAESAR: Cowards die many times before their deaths. The valiant never taste of death but once. Of all the things to fear, death is a strange one. It is a necessary end. It will come when it will come.

(Enter a servant.)

What did the priests say?

SERVANT: They want you to stay home. They looked through the insides of the animal sacrifice and could not find a heart.

CAESAR: The gods do this to shame me. I would be a beast without a heart if I stayed home today. No, I shall not. Danger and I were born on the same day. Caesar shall go forth.

CALPURNIA: Alas, my lord. Do not go out today. Say it was my fear that kept you home today, and not your own. We'll send Mark Antony today. He will say you are not well. I beg you on my knees.

CAESAR: Mark Antony shall say I am not well. To humor you, I will stay home.

(Enter Decius.)

	Here's Decius Brutus. He will tell them so.
DECIUS:	Caesar, all hail! I came to take you to the Senate House.
CAESAR:	Tell the Senate I will not come today.
CALPURNIA:	Say he is sick.
CAESAR:	Shall Caesar lie? Am I afraid to tell the truth, after all my conquests? Decius, go tell them Caesar will not come.
DECIUS:	Mighty Caesar, let me know some cause. I'm afraid they will laugh at me if I don't give them any reason.
CAESAR:	The cause is my will. I will not come. That is enough to satisfy the Senate. Because I love you, I will tell you. Calpurnia dreamed last night that my statue was covered with blood. It ran like a hundred fountains. Romans were smiling and washing their hands in the blood. She thinks this is a bad sign. On her knees, she begged me to not go out.
DECIUS:	This dream is misinterpreted. The Romans washing in your blood means that they are fed by your greatness. Your blood has revived Rome.
CAESAR:	That is well explained.
DECIUS:	You will know it is true when you hear what I have to say. The Senate has decided to give you a crown today. If you send word that you will not come, they might change their minds. Besides, they will mock you for staying home. They might say, 'Close down the Senate till Caesar's wife has better

dreams.' They might whisper 'is Caesar afraid?' But I tell you all this because I love you.

CAESAR: How foolish your dreams seem now, Calpurnia! I am ashamed I listened to you. Give me my robe. I will go.

(Enter Brutus, Ligarius, Metellus, Casca, Trebonius, Cinna, and Publius.)

And look. Here's Publius, come to fetch me.

PUBLIUS: Good morning, Caesar.

CAESAR: Good morning, Publius. Brutus, what are you doing up so early? Good morning, Casca, Caius Ligarius. What time is it?

BRUTUS: Caesar, it's already eight o'clock.

CAESAR: Thank you for your courtesy.

(Enter Antony.)

Look, here's Antony, who is up early even though he was up all night playing. Good morning, Antony.

ANTONY: The same to you, noble Caesar.

CAESAR: Good friends, go in and taste some wine with me. Then soon, we will all go together like friends.

BRUTUS: *(Aside.)* Oh, Caesar! It pains me to think that things are not always what they seem.

(All exit.)

Act II
Scene 3

(Enter Artemidorus, reading a paper.)

ARTEMIDORUS: *(Reading aloud.) Caesar, beware of Brutus. Take heed of Cassius. Don't go near Casca. Have an eye on Cinna. Trust not Trebonius or Metellus Cimber. Decius Brutus does not love you. You have wronged Caius Ligarius. There is but one mind of all these men and it is bent against Caesar. If you are not immortal, watch out for danger. Security gives way to conspiracy. The mighty gods defend you!*

> *One who loves you,*
> *Artemidorus.*

I will stand here until Caesar passes by. I will give him this note. My heart is sad that such virtue as Caesar's creates such rivalry. If you read this, Caesar, you may live. If not, fate is on the side of the traitors.

(Exits.)

Act II
Scene 4

(Enter Portia and Lucius.)

PORTIA: Boy, run to the Senate house. Don't answer me. Just go. What are you waiting for?

LUCIUS: To find out what you want me to do.

PORTIA: It would take me too long to explain to you what to do.

(Aside.)

Oh! That I may be strong! I have a man's mind but a woman's body. Are you still here, Lucius?

LUCIUS: Madam, what shall I do? Run to the Capitol? And then run back again?

PORTIA: Bring me word. Tell me if your master is well. He left here sickly. Also, let me know what Caesar does. Listen! What is that noise, boy?

LUCIUS: I hear nothing, madam.

(Enter the Soothsayer.)

PORTIA: Where have you been? Is Caesar gone to the Capitol yet?

SOOTHSAYER: Madam, not yet. I am on my way. I will stand and watch him pass by me.

PORTIA: You have some business with Caesar?

SOOTHSAYER: I do, if he will listen to me. I want to beg him to take care of himself.

PORTIA: Why? Are you aware of some danger to him?

SOOTHSAYER: Not that I know will happen. But some that I fear will happen. Good bye to you now.

PORTIA: I must go in. How weak is the heart of a woman. Oh, Brutus, may heaven speed up your business! Run, Lucius. Tell my lord that I am merry. Come back and tell me what he says to you in return.

            (Exit both.)

Act III
Scene 1

(Flourish. Enter Caesar, Brutus, Cassius, Casca, Decius, Metellus, Trebonius, Cinna, Antony, Lepidus, Artemidorus, Popilius, Publius, and the Soothsayer.)

CAESAR: The ides of March are come.

SOOTHSAYER: Ay, Caesar, but not gone.

ARTEMIDORUS: Hail Caesar! Read this document.

DECIUS: Trebonius asked you to look over this request, at your earliest convenience.

ARTEMIDORUS: Oh Caesar, read mine first. Mine is a request that concerns you personally. Read it, great Caesar!

CAESAR: I will read last the one that concerns me personally.

ARTEMIDORUS: Don't delay, Caesar. Read it instantly!

CAESAR: What! Is the fellow mad?

PUBLIUS: Sir, get out of the way!

CASSIUS: Don't bother Caesar with requests in the street. Come into the Capitol.

(Caesar goes into the Capitol. The rest follow.)

POPILIUS: I hope your business succeeds today.

CASSIUS:	What business, Popilius?
POPILIUS:	Farewell. *(Goes toward Caesar.)*
BRUTUS:	What did Popilius say?
CASSIUS:	He said he hopes our business today succeeds. I am afraid our plan has been discovered.
BRUTUS:	Look how he's going toward Caesar. Watch him.
CASSIUS:	Casca, be quick. We don't want to be delayed. Brutus, what shall we do?
BRUTUS:	Cassius, don't worry. Popilius is not talking to Caesar about our plan. He is smiling. Caesar's expression is not changing.
CASSIUS:	Trebonius is on time. Look, he's leading Mark Antony out of our way.
	(Exit Antony and Trebonius.)
DECIUS:	Where is Metellus Cimber? He should go right now to Caesar to present his request.
BRUTUS:	He is ready. Gather near him now.
CINNA:	Casca, are you the first to raise your hand?
CAESAR:	Are we all ready now? What is wrong now that Caesar and his Senate need to address?
METELLUS:	Most high and mighty Caesar. Metellus Cimber kneels before you with humble heart. *(Kneels.)*
CAESAR:	I cannot allow you to kneel. This kind of groveling might impress ordinary men. But I am not such a fool. Your brother was

banished. I will not change my mind. If you're going to beg like a dog, I will treat you like a dog. I will kick you out of my way. I made the right decision. I will not change.

METELLUS: Is there someone else who could convince you to change your mind?

BRUTUS: I kiss your hand, Caesar. I ask you to pardon Publius Cimber.

CAESAR: What, Brutus?

CASSIUS: Pardon, Caesar! I stand on my feet and beg for pardon for Publius Cimber.

CAESAR: I could be moved to change my mind, if I were like you. But I am as constant as the Northern Star. Men are weak and changeable. I only know one that is constant. I will not change my order that Cimber is banished.

CINNA: Oh, Caesar.

CAESAR: What! Will you raise the heavens to plead for Cimber?

DECIUS: Great Caesar!

CAESAR: Are you kneeling, too?

CASCA: Speak, hands, for me!

(They stab Caesar, Casca first, Brutus last.)

CAESAR: *Et tu, Brute?*—Then fall, Caesar.

(Dies.)

CINNA: Liberty! Freedom! Tyranny is dead! Run and cry it in the streets!

CASSIUS: Some of you go to the public speaking platforms. There call out: 'Peace, freedom, and liberty!'

BRUTUS: People and senators, don't be afraid. Don't run away. Caesar has paid the debt for his ambition.

CASCA: Go to the platform, Brutus.

DECIUS: And Cassius too.

BRUTUS: Where's Publius?

CINNA: He's here. He is completely confused by this mutiny.

METELLUS: Stick close together in case some friend of Caesar's should happen—

BRUTUS: Don't talk of organizing resistance. Publius, don't worry. There is no harm intended to you. Nor any other Roman. Tell the rest of them. Publius.

CASSIUS: Leave us, Publius. Avoid the crowds that might hurt you accidentally if they are trying to rush at us.

BRUTUS: That's right. And let no one take responsibility for this act but us.

(Enter Trebonius.)

CASSIUS: Where's Antony?

TREBONIUS: He fled to his house in shock. Men, women, and children are standing around in the streets. They are acting as if it were the end of the world.

BRUTUS: Fates, what have you planned for us? We know we will die someday. It's the question of when that bothers men.

CASCA: Yes. If you cut off twenty years of life, that's

twenty years you don't have to fear death.

BRUTUS: If you think of it that way, death is a good thing. So we are Caesar's friends and we did him a favor. Stoop here and bathe your hands in Caesar's blood. Smear it on your arms up to your elbows. Put it on your swords. Then we will go together to the Roman forum. We will wave our red swords in the air shouting, 'Peace, liberty and freedom!'

CASSIUS: Stoop and wash in the blood. How many times will this scene be acted out? It will be replayed in places not yet discovered. It will be acted in accents not yet heard.

BRUTUS: How many times will an actor playing Caesar bleed in plays?

CASSIUS: Each time that happens, they will call us the men that gave their country liberty.

DECIUS: Shall we go now?

CASSIUS: Ay, all of us will go. Brutus will lead the way. We, the boldest and best hearts of Rome will honor him.

(Enter a servant.)

BRUTUS: Who is that coming? A friend of Antony's.

SERVANT: My master, Mark Antony, told me to kneel before you. He said to tell you that Brutus is noble, wise, valiant, and honest. That Caesar was mighty, bold, royal and loving. He loves and honors Brutus. If Brutus will promise Antony's safety, he will come to him to hear why Caesar had to die. Then Antony will love the living Brutus more than the

101

dead Caesar. He will follow Brutus through his uncertain future.

BRUTUS: Your master is wise. Tell him to come. I promise he will leave unharmed.

SERVANT: I will fetch him right away. *(Exits.)*

BRUTUS: I know he will be a good friend to us.

CASSIUS: I wish that were so. But I have a bad feeling about him. And my feelings are generally right.

(Enter Mark Antony.)

BRUTUS: Welcome, Mark Antony.

ANTONY: Oh, mighty Caesar! Do you lie so low? Are all your glories and conquests shrunk to this? Farewell!

I don't know who else you intend to kill, gentlemen. But if you plan to kill me, now is the time. There is no better hour than the same one Caesar died. The hands and swords you used on Caesar are rich with noble blood. If I lived a thousand years, there would never be a better time or place for my death.

BRUTUS: Oh, Antony, don't beg us to kill you! Although our hands appear bloody and cruel now, you do not see our hearts. Caesar's wrongs made us hard to him. As to you, our hearts are full of love and kindness. Our swords have leaden points for you.

CASSIUS: Your vote will be the same as all of ours in matters of the state.

BRUTUS:	Just be patient. Let us first calm the crowd. Then I will explain to you why I had to kill Caesar, despite my love for him.
ANTONY:	I do not doubt your wisdom. Let me shake your bloody hands. First, Marcus Brutus, I shake your hand. Next Caius Cassius, I take your hand. Now, Decius Brutus, yours. Now yours, Metellus, yours, Cinna, and, my valiant Casca, yours. Last but not least, good Trebonius. Gentlemen, what can I say? I have no credibility. You must think I am a either a coward or a flatterer.
	Caesar, it's true: I did love you. If you can see me now, it must hurt you to watch me shaking the bloody hands of your enemies. I stand here with your corpse. If I had as many eyes as your wounds, I would weep as fast as they are bleeding. That would be better than this friendship with your foes. Pardon me, Julius! Here is where the hunters struck you down like a deer in the forest.
CASSIUS:	Mark Antony—
ANTONY:	Pardon me, Caius Cassius. Even Caesar's enemies will say as much. For a friend to say this is mild.
CASSIUS:	I don't blame you for praising Caesar so. But I want to know if we are to count on you as a friend, or not.
ANTONY:	That is why I shook hands with you. But I looked down and saw Caesar and became confused. I am friends with all of you. That is why I hope you will explain why Caesar

was dangerous.

BRUTUS: Our reasons are so good that if you were the son of Caesar, you would be satisfied.

ANTONY: That is all I ask. And one more request. That his body be brought to the marketplace. There I would like permission to speak at his funeral.

BRUTUS: You shall, Mark Antony.

CASSIUS: Brutus, a word with you. *(Aside to Brutus.)* You know not what you do. Do not consent that Antony speak at the funeral. Don't you know how much people will be moved by what he says?

BRUTUS: *(Aside to Cassius.)* I will speak first on the reason for Caesar's death. Then, I will also tell the people that we gave permission for Antony to speak. This will show that we are willing to give Caesar a regular funeral and honors. It will be to our advantage.

CASSIUS: *(Aside to Brutus.)* I know not what may fall, but I like it not.

BRUTUS: Mark Antony, take Caesar's body. Do not blame us in your funeral speech. Speak of the good Caesar did. And tell the people we gave you permission to speak. And I will speak first. You will follow me at the same place. You may speak if you agree with these conditions.

ANTONY: Be it so. I desire no more.

BRUTUS: Prepare the body then. And follow us.

(Exit all but Mark Antony.)

104

ANTONY: O pardon me, thou bleeding piece of earth. That I am meek and gentle with these butchers. You are the finest man that ever lived in history. Woe to those who shed your blood! A curse shall fall upon all of Italy. There shall be such a bloody civil war. Caesar's spirit shall be raging for revenge.

(Enter Octavius' servant.)

You are Octavius' servant, aren't you?

SERVANT: I am.

ANTONY: You are full of grief, I see. Your tears are making me cry. Is your master coming?

SERVANT: He is within seven leagues of Rome tonight.

ANTONY: Race back and tell him what happened. Tell him this is a dangerous Rome. It's not safe for him. I am going to take Caesar's body to the marketplace. There I will try to tell the people about this cruel deed. Stay and watch. Then report the results to Octavius. Lend me a hand with the body.

(Exit with Caesar's body.)

Act III
Scene 2

(Enter Brutus and Cassius with the plebians.)

PLEBIANS: We demand a full explanation!

BRUTUS: Then follow me and give me your attention, friends. Cassius, you go to the other street and take half the peoplc there. I will talk to those here.

PLEBIAN 1: I will hear Brutus speak.

PLEBIAN 2: I will go with Cassius. Then we will compare their reasons.

(Exit Cassius, with some of the plebians.)

PLEBIAN 3: The noble Brutus is ready. Silence!

BRUTUS: Romans, countrymen, and friends, hear me for reasons and be silent. You can believe what I say because you know me to be honorable. No one loved Caesar more than I. It's not that I loved Caesar less, but that I loved Rome more. Would you rather Caesar be alive and you all die as slaves? As Caesar loved me, I weep for him. As he was fortunate, I rejoice for him. As he was valiant, I honor him. But, as he was ambitious, I killed him. There are tears for his love, joy for his fortune, honor for his bravery, and death for his ambition.

(Enter Mark Antony and others with Caesar's body.)

Here comes his body, mourned by Mark Antony. He had no hand in Caesar's death. Still he receives the benefit of the death, citizenship in Rome, as each of you has. Now I leave you with this thought. As I killed my best friend for the good of Rome, I have the same dagger for myself when it shall please my country to need my death.

ALL: Live, Brutus! Live, live!

PLEBIAN 1: Bring him home in triumph to his house.

PLEBIAN 2: Put up a statue of Brutus.

PLEBIAN 3: Let him be Caesar.

PLEBIAN 4: The best of Caesar shall be crowned in Brutus.

PLEBIAN 1: We will bring him to his house with cheers.

BRUTUS: My countrymen—

PLEBIAN 2: Peace! Silence! Brutus speaks.

PLEBIAN 1: Peace.

BRUTUS: Good countrymen, show respect to Caesar's corpse by staying here to listen to Antony.

(Exit.)

PLEBIAN 1: Stay, let us hear Antony speak.

ANTONY: Brutus allowed me to speak.

(Antony goes to the platform.)

PLEBIAN 4: What does he say of Brutus?

PLEBIAN 3: He says that Brutus allowed him to speak.

PLEBIAN 4: He had better not say anything bad about Brutus.

PLEBIAN 1: Caesar was a tyrant!

PLEBIAN 3: That's certain. Rome is blessed to be rid of him.

PLEBIAN 2: Quiet. Let us hear what Antony has to say.

ANTONY: Friends, Romans, countrymen, lend me your ears! I come to bury Caesar, not to praise him. The evil that men do lives after them. The good is often interred with their bones. So, let it be with Caesar. The noble Brutus has told you that Caesar was ambitious. If true, that's a serious offense, and Caesar has paid for it by his death. So Brutus says, and Brutus is an honorable man. They are all honorable men.

Caesar was my faithful friend. But Brutus says he was ambitious. And Brutus is an honorable man.

Caesar filled up the public treasury with his triumphs. Does this seem ambitious? When the poor cried, Caesar wept. Ambition should be made of sterner stuff. Yet Brutus says he was ambitious. And Brutus is an honorable man. You all did see that on Lupercal, I tried to put the crown on his head. Three times I tried. Three times he refused it. Was that ambition? Still Brutus says he was ambitious. And Brutus is an honorable man. I do not speak to disprove what Brutus said. But here I am to speak what I do know. You all did love him once with good cause.

PLEBIAN 1:	I think there's sense in what he's saying.
PLEBIAN 2:	If you think about it, Caesar has been greatly wronged.
PLEBIAN 3:	I'm afraid worse rulers than he will take his place.
PLEBIAN 4:	Did you hear what he said? He wouldn't take the crown.
	Therefore he was not ambitious.
PLEBIAN 1:	If that's true, someone will have to pay for this.
PLEBIAN 2:	Poor soul! His eyes are red from weeping.
PLEBIAN 3:	There's not a nobler soul in Rome than Antony.
PLEBIAN 4:	Now watch. He speaks again.
ANTONY:	Here's a document I found among Caesar's things. It is his will. I won't read it. If you heard it, you would go and kiss his wounds.
PLEBIAN 4:	We will hear it! Read the will, Mark Antony.
ALL:	Read the will! We will hear Caesar's will!
ANTONY:	Be patient, gentle friends. I must not read it. Hearing the will of Caesar will inflame you.
PLEBIAN 4:	Read the will, Antony. We will hear Caesar's will.
ANTONY:	I fear I have wronged the honorable men who stabbed Caesar.
PLEBIAN 4:	They were traitors!
ALL:	The will!
PLEBIAN 2:	They were villains, murderers! Read the

will!

ANTONY: You insist that I read the will? Make a ring around the corpse of Caesar.

(Antony comes down.)

If you have tears, prepare to shed them now. Look at his toga. This is the place where Cassius' dagger ran through. See what a rip the malicious Casca made. Through this hole the beloved Brutus stabbed. Look how the blood rushed out of that hole. For Brutus, as you know, was Caesar's angel. How dearly Caesar loved him. This was the unkindest cut of all. For when Caesar saw Brutus stab him, his mighty heart burst.

PLEBIAN 1: Oh, piteous spectacle!

PLEBIAN 2: Oh, noble Caesar!

PLEBIAN 3: Oh, woeful day!

PLEBIAN 4: Oh, traitors, villains!

PLEBIAN 1: Oh, most bloody sight!

PLEBIAN 2: We will be revenged!

ALL Revenge! Burn! Fire! Kill! Let not a traitor live!

ANTONY: Stay, countrymen.

PLEBIAN 1: Peace. Hear the noble Antony.

PLEBIAN 2: We will hear him. We will follow him. We will die with him!

ANTONY: I am no orator as Brutus is. I'm just a simple man who loves his friend. That's why they allowed me to speak to you. I haven't the power to stir men's blood. I show you

110

Caesar's wounds and ask them to speak for me. Were I Brutus, then I could put a voice to each of Caesar's wounds. That voice would be powerful enough to move the stones of Rome to rise up and mutiny.

ALL   We'll mutiny!

PLEBIAN 1:   We'll burn the house of Brutus.

PLEBIAN 3:   Away. We will find the conspirators.

ANTONY: Friends, you don't yet know how much Caesar loved you. You forgot about the will.

ALL: Most true. The will! Let's stay and hear the will.

ANTONY: Here is the will. Caesar left to each and every Roman citizen seventy-five drachmas.

PLEBIAN 2:   Most noble Caesar! We'll revenge his death!

PLEBIAN 3:   Oh, royal Caesar!

ANTONY: He also left you all his walks, his gardens, his orchards. They are all for you to be used for public parks. Here was a Caesar! When comes another?

PLEBIAN 1:   Never, never! Come! We'll burn his body in the most holy place. With the fire, we'll torch the traitors' houses.

PLEBIAN 2:   Go fetch fire!

PLEBIAN 3:   Pull out benches for the fire!

PLEBIAN 4:   Pull out shutters, windows, anything!

               (Exit plebians with the body.)

ANTONY: Now let it work. Mischief, thou art afoot. Take what course thou will!

               (Servant enters.)

SERVANT: Sir, Octavius is already in Rome.

ANTONY: Where is he?

SERVANT: He and Lepidus are at Caesar's house.

ANTONY: I will go there at once to visit them.

SERVANT: I heard him say Brutus and Cassius are running like madmen through the gates of Rome.

ANTONY: They probably heard about the people, and how I moved them. Bring me to Octavius.

(Exit all.)

Act III
Scene 3

(Enter Cinna the poet, and after him the plebians.)

CINNA: I dreamed last night that I feasted with Caesar. In light of what has happened today, that's a bad sign.

PLEBIAN 1: What is your name?

PLEBIAN 2: Where are you going?

PLEBIAN 3: Where do you live?

PLEBIAN 4: Are you a married man or a bachelor?

CINNA: I am going to Caesar's funeral. I live near the Capitol.

My name is Cinna. I say I am a bachelor.

PLEBIAN 1: Tear him to pieces. He's a conspirator.

CINNA: I am Cinna the poet! I am Cinna the poet!

PLEBIAN 4: Tear him for his bad poetry. Tear him for his bad poetry.

CINNA: I am not Cinna the conspirator.

PLEBIAN 4: It doesn't matter. His name is Cinna. Kill him for his name, and keep on going.

PLEBIAN 3: Tear him! Tear him! *(They kill him.)* Come with the torches. To Brutus' and Cassius' houses! Burn all! Some go to

Decius' and some to Casca's. Some to Ligarius'. Go!

(All exit carrying the body of Cinna.)

Act IV

Scene 1

(Enter Antony, Octavius, and Lepidus.)

ANTONY: *(Looking over a list of names.)* These are the men who shall die.

OCTAVIUS: Your brother must die, Lepidus. Do you consent?

LEPIDUS: I do consent.

OCTAVIUS: Mark him down, Antony.

LEPIDUS: On condition that Antony's nephew, Publius, must die.

ANTONY: He shall not live. Look, with a spot I damn him. But, Lepidus, go to Caesar's house. Get the will. We will try to cut out some of these legacies.

LEPIDUS: Shall I find you here?

OCTAVIUS: Here or at the Capitol.

(Exit Lepidus.)

ANTONY: He is not worthy of us. He is only good for errands. Is it right that he should share equally the world, divided between us in three parts?

OCTAVIUS: But you allowed him equal vote with us, choosing who should die and who should live.

ANTONY: I am older and more experienced than you. We will use him while we need him.

OCTAVIUS: Do what you want. But he is a good soldier.

ANTONY: So is my horse. He is trained to do what he should. And for that reason, I provide for him. So consider him as property. Now listen, Brutus and Cassius are raising an army. We must use all our powers and all our resources to raise our own army. Let us go to the council to decide the best way to handle this.

OCTAVIUS: Yes, let us do that. For we are in danger right now. We have many enemies. There are also those who smile at us but have mischief on their minds.

(Both exit.)

Act IV
Scene 2

(Drum roll is heard. Enter Brutus, Lucilius, and the Army. Titinius and Pindarus meet them.)

BRUTUS: Is Cassius near?

LUCILIUS: He is near. And his servant Pindarus comes to give you greetings.

BRUTUS: Your master has given me some problems lately. But if he's here, he can explain.

PINDARUS: I am sure he has a good explanation for you. He is full of regard and honor.

BRUTUS: I do not doubt his honor.

(Brutus and Lucilius draw away.)

Tell me honestly, Lucilius. How did he receive you?

LUCILIUS: With courtesy and respect. But he wasn't as warm and friendly as in the past.

BRUTUS: Notice that when a friendship is cooling, people act more polite and formal. Is his army coming?

LUCILIUS: The army is camped in Sardis tonight. Cassius and the cavalry have come here.

(Enter Cassius and his generals.)

CASSIUS: Most noble brother, you have done me wrong.

BRUTUS: Cassius, speak softly. Don't let the troops see us arguing. They should see nothing but love between us. Come in my tent and tell me what is wrong.

CASSIUS: Pindarus, tell our commanders to lead the troops a short distance away from here.

(Exit all but Brutus and Cassius.)

Act IV

Scene 3

CASSIUS: You condemned Lucius Pella for taking bribes from the Sardians. This, after I wrote and told you to take his side.

BRUTUS: You wronged me by asking me such.

CASSIUS: In times like this, it is not good to criticize every little crime.

BRUTUS: Let me tell you this, Cassius. You yourself have been criticized for an itchy palm.

CASSIUS: I, an itchy palm? Lucky for you that you are Brutus. Or that would be your last speech.

BRUTUS: The name of Cassius honors corruption. For your good name hides the criticism.

CASSIUS: Criticism?

BRUTUS: Remember the ides of March. Didn't great Julius bleed for justice? Each of us stabbed at him for justice. And now, do we use those same hands for taking bribes? I'd rather be a dog and howl at the moon than such a Roman.

CASSIUS: Brutus, don't provoke me. I'll not endure it.

BRUTUS: Go away, worthless man!

CASSIUS: What are you saying?

BRUTUS:	Hear me, for I will speak. Must I give way to your temper? I am supposed to be frightened when you act like a mad man?
CASSIUS:	Oh, my god! Must I endure this?
BRUTUS:	All this and more! Go have a temper tantrum for your slaves. From now on I will laugh at your anger.
CASSIUS:	Even Caesar would not have spoken to me so badly.
BRUTUS:	You wouldn't have provoked him so.
CASSIUS:	Don't make me do something I will be sorry for.
BRUTUS:	You have already done that which you should be sorry for. I sent a message asking you for gold to pay my troops. You ignored me. I had no money to use. I cannot raise money by bribes. My honor is too great to squeeze money from the poor peasants like you do. I wouldn't have treated you so.
CASSIUS:	I denied you not.
BRUTUS:	You did.
CASSIUS:	I did not. The messenger was a fool. You have torn my heart apart. A friend should be blind to his friend's faults. But you have made mine larger than they are.
BRUTUS:	A flatterer would be blind to his friends' faults. Not a true friend.
CASSIUS:	Come, Antony and Octavius! Revenge yourself on Cassius. I am tired of living. My best friend hates me. Here is my dagger. Here is my heart. Stab me, Brutus, as you

did Caesar. For I know that when you hated him worst, you loved him more than you ever loved me.

BRUTUS: Stop now. I will forgive your angry comments. I was ill-tempered, too.

CASSIUS: Do you admit that? Give me your hand.

BRUTUS: And my heart, too.

CASSIUS: Have you not enough love to bear with me when my bad temper that my mother gave me makes me forget myself?

BRUTUS: Yes, Cassius, from now on when you lose your temper, I will think it is your mother. Lucius, a bowl of wine!

CASSIUS: I did not think that you could have been so angry.

BRUTUS: Oh, Cassius, I am sick of many griefs!

CASSIUS: You shouldn't worry about things you cannot control.

BRUTUS: Portia is dead.

CASSIUS: What, Portia? I am lucky you didn't kill me just now. What a terrible loss. How did it happen?

BRUTUS: She grieved that Antony and Octavius had made themselves so strong. She became depressed. And when her attendants were absent, she swallowed hot burning coals.

CASSIUS: And died that way?

(Enter Lucius with wine and candles.)

BRUTUS: Speak no more of her. Give me a bowl of wine. In this, I bury all unkindness,

Cassius.

(Drinks.)

CASSIUS: I drink to your love, Brutus. *(Drinks.)*

(Enter Titanius and Messala.)

BRUTUS: Messala, I have heard that Octavius and Mark Antony are coming with a mighty army toward Phillipi.

MESSALA: I have heard the same. I also heard that they put to death a hundred senators.

BRUTUS: I have heard it was only seventy senators that died, Cicero being one.

MESSALA: Have you had letters from your wife, my lord?

BRUTUS: No, Messala.

MESSALA: I think that strange.

BRUTUS: Why are you asking? Have you heard anything about her?

MESSALA: No, my lord.

BRUTUS: Tell me the truth as you are a Roman.

MESSALA: Like a Roman I bear the truth. For certain, she is dead and by strange manner.

BRUTUS: Farewell, Portia. We all must die, Messala.

MESSALA: Even so, great men endure great losses.

CASSIUS: My nature could not bear it so.

BRUTUS: Well, back to our work. What do you think of marching to Phillippi?

CASSIUS: I don't think it is a good idea. It's better that the enemy come to us. That way, he will be tired and worn out by the time he arrives.

BRUTUS: However, he may gain additional soldiers from the people of Philippi as he marches. Those people are not too fond of us. They may aid and join forces with Antony's troops. I think we better face him at Philippi.

CASSIUS: Listen to me, my brother.

BRUTUS: There's another reason. We've used up all our resources. Our armies are full. The enemy increases every day. There is a tide in the affairs of men which, taken at the flood, leads on to fortune. Omitted, all the voyage of their life is bound in shallows and in miseries. We must go now or lose the current when it serves or lose our ventures.

CASSIUS: Then we will go and meet them at Philippi. Oh, dear brother, let us never argue as we did this night.

BRUTUS: All is well. Goodnight, good brother.

(Exit all but Brutus. Enter Lucius, Varo and Claudius.)

BRUTUS: I pray you, sirs, lie in my tent and sleep. I may need you to run errands tonight. If so I will wake you.

VARO: We will stay awake and wait your command.

BRUTUS: I will not have it. Now lie down, good sirs. Maybe later you will need to stay awake. *(Varo and Claudius lie down.)* Lucius, can I trouble you to play the lute awhile?

LUCIUS: Yes, if it pleases you. *(Plays a short while and then falls asleep.)*

BRUTUS:	This is a sleepy tune. I won't wake him. I will read my book.
	(Enter the ghost of Caesar.) Ha! Who comes here? I think my eyes are weak. Are you a devil? An angel? Some god? Speak! Who are you to make my blood run cold and my hair stand on end?
GHOST:	Thy evil spirit, Brutus. I have come to tell you that you will see me at Philippi.
BRUTUS:	Well, I will see you at Philippi, then. *(Exit Ghost.)* Now that I have my courage, you have vanished.
	(Lucius, Varo, and Claudius awake.) Did you cry out in your sleep?
LUCIUS:	No, my lord.
VARO:	Not I, my lord.
BRUTUS:	Did you see anything?
CLAUDIUS:	Nothing, my lord.
BRUTUS:	Go and tell Cassius to advance early in the morning. We will follow him.
VARO:	It shall be done. *(Exit all.)*

Act V

Scene 1

(Enter Octavius, Antony, and their Army.)

OCTAVIUS: Now, Antony, our hopes are answered. You said the enemy would not come down. But here they are at Philippi. They are challenging us before we chased them down.

ANTONY: I know they would rather hide from us. But they think this show of bravery will scare us.

MESSENGER: Prepare, Generals. The enemy has put out the red flag for battle. We need to act quickly.

ANTONY: Octavius, lead your army slowly on the left side of the field.

OCTAVIUS: I should be on the right side and you on the left.

ANTONY: Why do you argue with me at this important moment?

OCTAVIUS: I do not argue with you, yet. But I will.

(March. Drum. Enter Brutus, Cassius and their army; Lucilius, Titinius, Messala, and others.)

BRUTUS: They want to talk before we begin the battle.

CASSIUS:	Hold on, Titinius, we have to talk with them.
OCTAVIUS:	Mark Antony, shall we give the sign of battle?
ANTONY:	No, Octavius, we will begin when they begin. Go and talk with them.
OCTAVIUS:	Don't move till the signal is given.
BRUTUS:	Words before blows. Is that it, countrymen?
OCTAVIUS:	Not that we love words better, as you do.
BRUTUS:	Good words are better than bad strokes, Octavius.
ANTONY:	You have used good words while using bad strokes at the same time. You made holes in Caesar's heart, while saying, 'Long live Caesar.'
CASSIUS:	Antony, we don't yet know how good your strokes are. But your words rob the bees of their honey.
ANTONY:	But they don't rob the bees of their stingers.
BRUTUS:	Yes, and you've robbed the bees of their buzzing. Wisely, you warn before you sting.
ANTONY:	Villains! You didn't warn Caesar when your vile daggers hacked into him. You grinned and bowed and kissed his feet. Meanwhile, Casca snuck behind him like a dog and struck him in the neck.
CASSIUS:	If I had my way, you wouldn't have been left alive to speak today. It's thanks to Brutus you are here.
OCTAVIUS:	Let's get down to business. We're sweating from this argument. The battle will turn our

sweat to redder drops. Look, my sword is drawn against conspirators. I will not sheathe my sword till Caesar's thirty-three wounds are avenged. Or until I, Octavius Caesar, have also died by the traitors' swords.

BRUTUS: Octavius, you cannot die by traitors' swords, unless you brought traitors with you.

OCTAVIUS: I was not born to die on Brutus' sword.

BRUTUS: You couldn't ask for a more honorable death.

CASSIUS: He is just a schoolboy, worthless of honor.

ANTONY: Still the same old Cassius.

OCTAVIUS: Come, Antony, let us go. Traitors! Come fight us today if you dare. If not, come when you have the guts.

(Exit Octavius, with Antony and army.)

(Brutus and Lucilius talk apart from the rest.)

CASSIUS: Messala!

MESSALA: What says my general?

CASSIUS: Messala, this is my birthday. You are my witness. Against my will, I am forced to go to risk all our freedom on one battle.

Noble Brutus, if we do lose this battle, then this is the last time we will speak. If we lose, will you surrender and be dragged through the streets of Rome?

BRUTUS: I hate to think of suicide. It seems so cowardly to cut short the time left for fear of what might happen. But do not think I will ever go as a captive to Rome. Today we end what was started on the ides of March. Whether we will ever meet again, I don't know. So, farewell, Cassius.

CASSIUS: Farewell, Brutus, forever!

(Exit all.)

Act V

Scene 2

(Sounds of alarm. Enter Brutus and Messala.)

BRUTUS: Ride, Messla, ride. Give these orders to the legions on the other side. It seems like Octavius' side has lost their spirit. These orders will overthrow him. Let the whole army come down.

(Both exit.)

Act V

Scene 3

(Sounds of alarm. Enter Cassius and Titinius.)

CASSIUS: Oh, look, Titinius, my own army is leaving! My own men have turned into my enemies. I had to kill the flag bearer who tried to run away.

TITINIUS: Oh, Cassius, Brutus gave the orders too early. His soldiers thought they had already won. They left us unprotected, and Antony surrounded us.

(Enter Pindarus.)

PINDARUS: Run, my lord! Mark Antony is here in camp.

CASSIUS: This hill is far enough. Look, our tents are on fire! Titinius, ride as fast as you can up to those troops. Then come back quickly and tell me if they are ours or enemy troops.

(Exit Titinius.)

CASSIUS: Go, Pindarus, get higher on the hill. Tell me what you see of Titinius. I am nearsighted.

(Pindarus goes up.)

CASSIUS: My life has run its compass. My time has come back to where life started.

(Pindarus shouts from above.)

PINDARUS: Oh, my lord! Titinius is surrounded by horsemen. Now they are upon him. Now they have taken him. They are shouting for joy.

CASSIUS: Come down. What a coward I am, that I should live to see my best friend taken. *(Pindarus comes down.)* Pindarus, I took you prisoner in Parthia. When I spared your life, I made you promise you would do anything I asked. Now, I free you. Take this sword that killed Caesar, and kill me. *(Pindarus stabs him.)* Caesar, thou art avenged, even with the sword that killed you.

PINDARUS: So, I am free. It was not my will to kill you, Oh, Cassius. I will run away to some country where Romans will not notice me. *(Exits.)*

(Titinius and Messala enter.)

TITINIUS: Cassius will be glad to know that Brutus is defeating Octavius' army. So it doesn't matter that Antony is defeating Cassius' army.

MESSALA: Isn't that Cassius lying on the ground up there?

TITINIUS: He looks like he is dead! Oh, my heart! He is dead. The sun of Rome has set. He died because he thought we were lost.

MESSALA: Why did he have to make such a mistake? It cost him his life. Go and look for Pindarus. I will bring this tragic news to Brutus.

(He exits.)

131

TITINIUS: Poor Cassius! Didn't I go forward and greet my friends? Didn't you hear the happy shouts? Why did you misunderstand everything? Here is the victory wreath that Brutus gave me for you. You shall wear it now. When Brutus comes, he will see how I honored Cassius. Come, sword, and find my heart.

(Dies, stabbing himself. Alarms sound. Enter Brutus, Messala, Young Cato, and others.)

BRUTUS: Oh, Julius Caesar! You still have power here! You make us turn our swords into our own bodies. Look, both Titinius and Cassius are dead! Rome shall not have such fine men as these again. Friends, I owe more tears than I can shed now. I will find time later. We shall not bury him here. We will send his body to Thasos for burial. Come, Cato, Lucilius. It is three o'clock and we shall go to battle a second time.

(Exit all.)

Act V

Scene 4

(Alarms sound. Enter Brutus, Messala, Young Cato, Lucilius, and Flavius.

BRUTUS: Countrymen, hold up your heads!

(Exit Messala and Flavius.)

CATO: I am Marcus Cato! I am a friend to my country and a foe to tyrants! Who will go with me?

(Enter soldiers and fight.)

BRUTUS: And I am Marcus Brutus. I am my country's friend!

(Exit Brutus)

(Young Cato falls.)

LUCILIUS: Oh, young and noble Cato, are you down? Now you die as bravely as Titinius. You will be honored, being Cato's son.

SOLDIER 1: Surrender or die!

LUCILIUS: I only surrender to die. I am Brutus. I will be honored in death.

SOLDIER 1: We must not kill him. He will be a noble prisoner.

(Enter Antony.)

SOLDIER 2: Run and tell Antony that Brutus is taken.

SOLDIER 1: I will tell him. Here he comes. Brutus is taken, my lord!

ANTONY: Where is he?

LUCILIUS: He is safe. I assure you that no enemy shall ever take Brutus alive. The gods defend him from so great a shame.

ANTONY: This is not Brutus. But he is still a prize. Keep him safe. Show him kindness. I would rather have him as a friend than an enemy. Go and see whether Brutus is alive or dead. Bring word to us in Octavius' tent.

(All exit.)

Act V

Scene 5

(Enter Brutus, Dardanius, Clitus, Strato and Volumnius.)

BRUTUS: Come, poor survivors. Rest on this rock. *(Whispers to Clitus.)*

CLITUS: No, my lord. Not for all the world would I do such a thing. I would rather kill myself.

BRUTUS: Dardanius, listen. *(Whispers to Dardanius.)*

DARDANIUS: Would I do such a thing?

BRUTUS: Volumnius, come here. The ghost of Caesar has appeared to me twice. Once was at Sardis. Once was here at Philippi fields. I know my time has come.

VOLUMNIUS: No, my lord.

BRUTUS: I am sure it is so. You see, our enemies have beaten us to the grave. It is more noble that we should jump in than wait till they push us in. You and I have been friends since we went to school together. For the sake of our friendship, hold my sword while I run into it.

VOLUMNIUS: That's not a job to ask a friend to do.

(Alarms sound.)

CLITUS: Run, my lord!

BRUTUS: Farewell to all of you. My heart is glad that in my whole life, my friends were true to me. I shall have more glory in losing this day than Antony shall have in winning. For he is destroying the Republic of Rome. I am tired and ready to die.

CLITUS: Run, my lord!

BRUTUS: Go ahead. I will follow.

(Exit Clitus, Dardanius, and Volumnius.)

Strato, you stay. You are a good servant. Hold my sword and look away while I run on it. Will you?

STRATO: Give me your hand first. Farewell, my lord.

BRUTUS: Caesar, now be still. I killed not thee with half so good a will.

(He runs into his sword and dies. Enter Octavius, Antony, Messala, Lucilius, and the Army.)

STRATO: Brutus is free now. Only Brutus defeated Brutus. No man gains honor from his death.

ANTONY: This was the noblest Roman of them all. All of the rest of the conspirators acted out of envy. Only Brutus honestly thought he was doing the deed for the good of all Romans.

OCTAVIUS: We shall give him a proper burial according to his high rank. Within my tent his bones tonight shall lie. Most like a soldier, ordered honorably. So call the field to rest, and let's away. To part the glories of this happy day.

(Exit all.)

THE GLOBE THEATER

The Globe Theater may well be the most famous theater in the world, for it was here that Shakespeare and other literary giants of his day produced their plays and other dramatic works.

Shakespeare and several other well-known actors needed a place to perform and so they pooled their funds and designed and built the Globe in 1599. Since they were theatrical professionals in every sense of the word, the building fit their needs perfectly. The Globe was octagonally-shaped with a roofless inner pit into which the stage projected. Three galleries (balconies) rose one above the other, the topmost of which had a thatched roof. One day, in order to provide reality in a production of Shakespeare's *King Henry the Eighth*, a cannon was discharged. Unfortunately, this piece of stagecraft set fire to the thatched roof, and the entire building burned. It was rebuilt the following year but was torn down by the Puritans 30 years later to make space for houses.

A few years ago, The Globe Theater was rebuilt, and now houses performances of Shakespeare's and other plays.

About the Editors

Peggy L. Anderson, PhD, is a professor and Special Education Program Coordinator at Metropolitan State College of Denver. She has taught students with learning disabilities at the elementary and middle school levels in South Carolina and Florida. Her master's degree is from the Citadel and her doctorate is from the University of Denver. She completed her postdoctoral work with the Department of Pediatrics at Johns Hopkins University. Her research interests have focused on language-learning disabilities, dyslexia, and inclusion issues.

Judith D. Anderson, JD, is a trial attorney in southern California, specializing in the defense of school districts. She has taught Shakespeare to high school students in the United States and the United Kingdom for ten years. As a Fullbright Scholar, she travelled extensively in the British Isles, and met with the Queen Mother of England. She received her bachelor's degree at Flagler College and her law degree at Southwestern University School of Law.